Heaven and Hell

Wallace and Bentley Series

Ashley De La O

ISBN: 979-8-89212-059-3

To my daughter, Scarlett De La O

About the Author

Born in Tarzana, California, Ashley grew up as a quote, "valley girl" in the San Fernando Valley. She attended Cal State University Northridge, graduating in 2008 with a Bachelor of Arts in Liberal Studies with a concentration in Women's Studies. Ashley met the love of her life, raised two dogs, and is currently co-parenting a daughter. A proud mom and advocate, in her free time, she also loves writing and her quiet life with her family.

Preface

In a world where the extraordinary often hides in the simplest of forms, there exists a belief that dogs are more than just loyal companions. Rather, they are sent to earth as angels who embody boundless love and devotion. In the eyes of some, they are sent to Earth as celestial beings who are born with fur coats, adorable eyes, and a cute wet snout.

This is the tale of two of these angels whose unwavering loyalty to their Mama and Papa would transcend the ordinary form of love. These dogs were entrusted with a mission: to become the embodiment of joy and love. They held a steadfast determination to bring joy to the lives of those around them. This is a heartwarming story of familial love and unity and the joy they brought to their owners' lives. Mama and Papa gave them love and rescued them from a life of challenges.

Bentley and Wallace were not just ordinary pets; they were the guardians of the positive. They would light up their parents' sometimes dark world. Their wagging tails and affectionate licks were proof of the profound love they carried within them. Their eyes sparkled with a depth of emotion that words cannot explain.

Join us in the following pages as we embark on a journey through the remarkable lives of these two dogs and the steadfast bonds they formed with the family they were sent to love. These canine angels weaved a tale of love and unity with their human family. They were companions, the ones with whom you could cuddle and feel your heart becoming whole again.

Through the highs and lows, the challenges and triumphs, the bond between these angels and their families grew every day. From the day Roy brought Wallace home till the day Wallace peacefully passed away, he remained a healer and confidant.

We venture into the remarkable lives of Wallace and Bentley as they tell us the story of the humans they swore to love and protect. Through laughter and tears, through moments of sheer bliss and times of heartache, their story serves as a testament to their power of love. The following pages will teach us that extraordinary joy can be found in the simplest of forms, especially with these furry companions.

Contents

Chapter 1: Street Dog to Family Dog

It was a cold smoggy afternoon in the 818. There was an alley beside an old bar where old men and women came to drink and throw their worries away. There were occasional fights in the bar. One night two young men got into a quarrel because of a girl and broke each other's noses. There I was in the alleyway, gleefully watching the fight unfold.

'Get 'em!' I thought to myself.

The first guy called a group of guys who trotted after him outside. They cornered the other guy and pinned him against the grimy wall. There were a bunch of profanities hurled between the two boys before the first guy lost it and punched the second guy straight in the jaw. The second guy grabbed his face as he fell.

"You stole my girl!" he yelled.

"She was my girl first!"

The second guy saw his chance and kicked the first one in the shin. The first guy let out a cry of surprise and fell to the ground. The second one got his chance and got on top of the first guy. He landed a blow to his nose. There was a sickening crack and blood started to flow down his face from his now broken nose.

I stood there, transfixed. Man, I sure did love watching humans get into their stupid fights. And at a bar, the probability of one happening was more likely.

I often wondered what it is like to be drunk. Humans talked about how fun it is but by the looks of this fight, it didn't work very well, did it?

Many a night I watched these quarrels. Most times girls dressed in pretty clothes would run to the alley to puke their guts out. 'How is this fun?' I would think to myself. 'Why do humans subject themselves to such destructive vices? They sure are peculiar creatures.'

Finally, the fight was over. Both boys rolled around on the ground in pain. The first guy's posse picked him up and dragged him back inside the bar. Most likely a sad attempt to nurse his injuries or take him to the hospital.

I felt sorry for the second guy as well. 'Could I help in some way?' I thought to myself but given the boy's condition, it didn't look like he would appreciate help from a mere animal. So I decided against it and walked toward a dumpster. The groaning of the boy faded into the background.

'How do I get inside?' I thought to myself. My eyes landed on a bunch of stacked cardboard boxes. 'Hmmm.'

I jumped up on the boxes and sniffed the contents of the dumpster, trying to get a whiff of some food. All

I smelled were some dirty socks and unwashed underwear. 'Ugh,' I thought.

So far, no luck. However, I didn't give up hope. There were many other dumpsters in the area. I didn't want to give up yet.

The dogs and cats were fighting in the streets, the roaches were breeding and here I was, scrounging around in the trash looking for garlic bread scraps. An old woman threw her apple core but I was too quick. I jumped up, grabbed it mid-air, and began chewing on the small rotting apple. This was a new low for me. Oh well, beggars can't be choosers.

I had just been kicked out of the Tantalizing Terrier club for being too good-looking and picking fights. I had a slight angry streak and I found myself involved in many tussles. I was opinionated and loved having my way. That's probably why I enjoyed watching people fight as well. I walked around the neighborhood, watching the cars pass by, their lights and the neon signs lighting up the night. They grew even brighter in the background of the night. A man walked past me and attempted to kick me. I yelped and jumped away just in time, dodging his kick.

'What a jerk,' I thought to myself.

It was hopeless. I hung my head and walked through the crowded streets, barely dodging humans as they bustled past me.

“Watch it, Mutt,” said a woman as she walked by me.

‘Thank you,’ I thought to myself and rolled my eyes.

I turned into another alley. No dumpsters.

‘Great.’

I finally found a cardboard box lying on its side. This was going to be my place to sleep for the night. I sighed, thinking, ‘Yet another night with no food.’

Just as I was trotting over, dizzy because of how hungry I was, a car passed me in speed, it’s loud horn making me jump. As my heart pounded in my chest, I realized that I almost got run over. Before I could collect myself, I felt a pair of arms go around my belly and my legs were lifted up into the air. To my shock, I was being picked up. I looked up to see a kind-looking woman smiling down at me. By the look of her hair caked up with dirt and lines of more dirt on her face, she seemed homeless. She was bug-eyed and they had deep dark circles underneath them, but her smile was gentle.

"Hey, I have your dog!" she yelled to a handsome young man with dark hair. He whipped around to see who was calling him. When his eyes met mine, his dark brown eyes stared softly through his designer black-rimmed glasses.

He was wearing black pants and a black hoodie with a bunch of skulls and roses on the front. He was a chubby handsome Latino man with shiny black hair which stuck out awkwardly. His eyes went from the woman's face down to me. His face broke out in a grin.

Now, miracles, you know, don't happen every day, especially for poor street dogs like me but he grabbed me and looked into my eyes. "I'm going to take you home with me little guy," he spoke gently, still grinning.

'Home?' I thought to myself. 'What's a home?'

He then put me in his old grand Jeep Cherokee blasting some ridiculous metal music. It was just a bunch of angry humans who decided to make sounds together.

"Korn, little boy?" he asked looking behind to check on me. I realized he was trying to ask me if I listened to the absurd music. He laughed to himself and turned his key in the ignition. "It's going to be okay, boy," he said kindly to me.

The guy was chewing Jack in the Box loudly out of a bag. He threw me a French fry in the back seat. I caught it in my mouth. I was grateful for the warm, tasty bite. I felt a calmness as I chewed the little salty fry. The guy drove for a good while before I felt his Jeep slow down and come to a stop.

'Where am I going?' I wondered to myself. 'I hope this guy doesn't turn out to be a total psycho.'

Opening the door, he grabbed me and took me inside a forlorn-looking gray apartment building and ran inside holding me.

"Don't worry, little man. I've got you. Let's get you some food."

My ears perked up at that.

"That's right, boy. You must be famished. Poor little dude. I'm going to take care of you and give you a warm bed to sleep in."

'Bed?' I wondered. 'What the heck is that?'

He opened the door to what would become my new home. Inside was a World Market-style apartment, vintage brown pieces of exotic furniture. A red and black satanic kitchen with funky red, brown, and orange colors on the walls. It had a living room and dining room. The guy threw me on the couch and ran toward the back of the house "Ashley, come here, I have a surprise!"

A petite, short, blond, and beautiful woman came out of the room with a look of surprise on her face. She was holding the most demonic-looking poodle I had ever seen. He had a skull bandana around his neck, his fur covered his eyes, and he had the most menacing underbite. He looked like he hadn't been groomed in months. 'Ew,' I thought to myself. But then again, I probably had some matting in my fur and dirt penetrating my white coat. I desperately needed a bath but so did the degenerate demon.

'How does he even see with all that hair?' I thought.

The woman gently set the other dog down. "Well, hello!" she said as she bent down to talk to me.

I knew exactly what I needed to do at that moment. I ran off the couch and picked a fight with the evil poodle. I jumped up on him, knocking him to the floor. I barked loudly and bared my teeth at the demon who yelped and started to cry. He didn't even try to fight back.

'What a coward.'

The woman screamed, "Roy, what the hell!?"

I felt bad instantly and knew that was a bad move. I looked at the poodle demon and saw him whimper. He ran back to the woman named Ashley and hid behind her shins.

I still needed to assert my dominance so I scratched her legs crying to pick me up but she had already picked up the demon dog.

"Bad dog!" she scolded me.

I winced and retreated a few steps.

Roy came behind me and scooped me up. "We don't attack others in this house, little man."

I looked up in his eyes apologetically. I still disliked the demon but I suppose I could treat it with a little more respect. I didn't want to go back to those cold, dirty alleys and have nothing to eat. Just the thought of being outside of this warm and cozy place was unbearable. I felt a certain peace unlike I had experienced before.

Gone were the days when humans tried to kick me or shun me out of the way. There was also a particularly mean cat who prowled through the neighborhood. His name was Rufus. He was a mangy black cat with long whiskers and white ears. He and his gang of evil cats would attack me from time to time. I was afraid of him.

Rufus was a bully. Just the thought of being picked on by Rufus made me shudder. He even smelled bad. Like rotting fish and poo. I don't know what I ever did to him but I suppose he just didn't need a reason to be a terror but cats are born that way.

Come to think of it, in a battle between a small dog of my size and a bunch of cats, the cats would definitely win. They had their murder weapons attached to their feet. One swat and you're whimpering and running back to whence you came. There was just something about the way they pulled their ears back and hissed that is genuinely so terrifying to me.

The woman called the little monster Bentley. “Oh, my poor baby Bentley. Did the bad doggo hurt you?” She cooed at him asking him if he was okay. She then handed him to the handsome chubby man. She looked at me angrily like I just harmed her child. She scoffed annoyed and picked me up in her arms. I started shaking scared I messed things up and would be back on the streets any minute. I sadly licked her beautiful hand crying. I looked up into her eyes and gave her my most sincere apologetic expression in hopes of deterring her anger. She seemed to melt immediately. Her brows which were furrowed now softened and relaxed.

"Look at our new dog, Ashley. Some woman gave him to me it was so weird. He's black and white just like Bentley " Roy tried to calm down her anger.

That was true, no matter how much I hated it. This poodle and I strangely looked like we were brothers. ‘Ew, do I look like that?’ I wondered to myself. I guess I should look in a mirror asap to determine whether that was true. I knew I was a handsome fellow since I have always been popular with the ladies. A lot of dogs in my area were clearly jealous of me too.

"Well, he *is* really cute," the woman said softly, her eyes still angry. "I guess we can keep him if he doesn't try to kill Bentley again. What should we name him?"

"I don't know, we'll think of something," Roy said chewing the rest of the Jack in the box.

"Ummm, help me out here," said Ashley. "How about Chance?"

I hated that name. 'Please don't name me that, please don't name me that,' I prayed, closing my eyes.

On the flat-screen TV was playing the movie "Scott Pilgrim vs the World."

"How about Wallace from Scott Pilgrim!" Roy yelled from the dining table. "Man, what a cool movie," he said.

Ashley turned to him excitedly "Yes, perfect! That sounds like a good name. I love it."

"Phew."

Then she said the most beautiful words I have ever heard; "Welcome to our family, Wallace! I am your Mama and he is your Papa."

It was one of the best days of all our lives including that annoying poodle Bentley's. I knew I had to behave with him even though I didn't really like him. I guess I didn't have much of a choice. The thought of me belonging somewhere and having a family was too good an opportunity to pass on.

Mama and Papa gave me some boiled chicken in a bowl. It was delicious. I hadn't had chicken in ages. This was the first time I had ever consumed a warm meal in my life. The sensation of the warm, chewy chicken in my mouth was heavenly. I felt a wave of pleasure pass through my body and my tail immediately began to wag. I gobbled down the food and let out a little, "ruff!" to thank them. I loved seeing them both smile down at me. I was glad that Mama didn't look angry anymore. I ran to her and lay my head on her lap.

"Awww," she said and stroked my head affectionately. "You're a good boy, aren't you?" she cooed.

Bentley the degenerate poodle was observing me from afar and was too scared to come near me. 'Good.' I thought to myself. 'Stay away from me.' I was sure he was jealous of my good looks too. I was particularly happy about the fact that he probably hated that Mama was paying attention to me instead of him.

The couple then put down a couple of blankets and put me on top of them. It was soft and warm. I felt myself sinking deep into the blankets. The warm glow of their bedside lamp gave me a sense of calm. There were no loud sounds and I was not used to such quiet. Before I knew it, I had drifted off to sleep.

Chapter 2: Our Glory Days

I was truly living my best life. From the harsh, cold, and wet streets, I was suddenly transferred to a warm and comfortable house. I was eating delicious food and didn't have to starve every day like I used to. Much to my annoyance, though, I had to share all of my blessings with that other dog living in the same house. Although I was slowly growing used to his presence, I felt territorial of my new blessings. Papa took great care of us, too, getting both of us matching spiked collars with a little license that had our names on it too.

Mama, on the other hand, would get us the best of the best food from Kahoots, a pet store not too far from my new home. The drive down there in her 2008 Toyota Matrix would be my favorite, where I would keep my head out of the window and feel the cold air hit my face. I also loved to pee in all the stores. Much to my surprise, Bentley peed like a girl, so I had to quickly teach him how to lift his leg and pee like a real man. Something about the whole ordeal made me feel like an elder brother toward Bentley, but I couldn't get myself to like him, which I felt was a pretty mutual feeling. He would sneak in and out of the house from time to time unnoticed by Mama and Papa.

There was one more problem, too: Evil Grandma. She lived next store and was our pseudo-apartment manager, interfering in all of our activities. Papa, Mama, and the family all had cheap apartments as the owner was a nice Jewish couple that gave all of Grandma's family and friends discounts. Mama and Papa's friends would always reach out. Some did take the opportunity for a cheap apartment. Uncle Ronnie and Carol, who lived in Auntie Nora's apartment two doors down, moved in the same time as Mama and Papa also benefiting from the generous discount. Although Bentley loved Aunt Nora as she sounded like Mama, I wasn't too fond of her since she always seemed to have it out for Mama. Dogs can sense these things.

Grandma and little sister Bailey would also always storm in unannounced, commenting on every detail of the house and asking Mama to make changes to their liking. One would think it's their house instead of Mama and Papa's. I always hated even the thought of them coming over. One day things took a turn for the better though. It was a beautiful morning when she suddenly started banging at the door, her impatience as annoying as ever. Mama rushed to open it, and Bentley and I stiffened in annoyance. Bentley also got up from the couch and ran to hide on top of the cupboard.

"Lucky demon," I thought to myself.

However, as Mama opened the door and let the old lady inside, I noticed a small beautiful dog, a Maltese with long white hair and a pink bow, to be accurate, following Evil Grandma inside. It was like time had stopped as I watched the beautiful canine walk into our apartment. It was truly love at first sight. As she walked inside, I felt compelled to make my way toward her; a feeling I had never felt before ran through my body. Unfortunately, as I closed into her, a huge hurdle came in the right between us. It was Evil Grandma.

"Get this loser away from my beautiful Lexi!" she shrieked in anger, signaling Mama to come to pick me up.

"Lexi... what a beautiful name..." I thought to myself.

I realized suddenly that Lexi wasn't even looking in my direction as her gaze remained focused on Bentley. A pang of jealousy filled my heart, and I decided to make my way to Lexi and confront her myself. Before I could reach my maiden in the hands of the evil witch who hated me and Papa, she grabbed the beautiful canine and then stormed out to go back to her apartment. My heart sank as I realized I had to find a way to get to her as soon as I could. I told Bentley I needed his help since he and Mama lived with Grandma before me and Papa came into the picture.

"Bentley, my dear best friend, you're looking awfully tough and menacing today," I told him as I tried to butter him up and hoped to find out if he was also in love with her like me.

"Thank you, Wallace..." Bentley replied, looking at me suspiciously. We had grown oddly fond of each other over time, but I wasn't ever as nice to him as I was right now.

"I'll be honest, Bentley... I need your help."

"I figured out that much... what do you want?"

"I think I just fell madly in love with Lexi, and I need you to introduce us as soon as possible," I told Bentley, carefully seeing how he responded.

"And why would I do that?" Bentley asked chewing items he found in the trash in the most nonchalant manner. He loved eating old paper towel rolls and licking the wrappers, anything that felt fun for his teeth to dig into. He loved taking weird items hiding them under his bed, and then growling at Mama and Papa when they tried to clean them. He was a strange canine.

"Well... because we are best friends, and I want Lexi to be mine!" I protested, hoping he would agree.

"I mean, I don't mind," Bentley got up and stretched his legs, "But then again, your biggest problem will be Grandma, who is not going to let that happen."

"Oh..." I responded half-heartedly.

"But I'll do my best for you, Wallace," he said, yawning, and started walking toward the door.

My heart softened as I realized that Bentley was surprisingly a very loving dog and friend, although he had his violent quirks. He definitely saw my love for Lexi and understood how badly I wanted to be with her.

"Thank you, Bentley. I can't tell you how much this means to me! You will be my best man and the godfather of my children!"

"Thank you very much, but I already have enough Wallaces' in my life!" He jumped to open the door with his teeth. "Let's go."

Grandma's apartment unit was next door to ours. Bentley and I quietly walked over and peeked inside the front door, which, luckily enough, was unlocked. Grandma was watching her favorite soap opera and gossiping, as always, on the phone with some crazy family member. Much to our surprise, even the screen door was open, so we decided to sneak inside. Bentley led the way, and I followed him, trying to be as silent as possible, but my nails hit the tiled floor with each step I took.

"Quietly, Wallace! Good thing we are black and white, so we at least match these tiles. We'll go in through the hallway; Grandma keeps Lexi in one of those dog cages in the bedroom..."

"In a cage? Oh, poor Lexi!" I empathized with my maiden in distress.

I felt beyond nervous as I followed Bentley to the bedroom, shaking at the thought of getting caught. Grandma hated me, but I wouldn't let her come between my true love, like Papa and Mama. At the end of the hall, we saw the bedroom door and hoped that it would be unlocked. As we reached the wooden frame, we noticed the door was ajar, and I wanted to jump with happiness. Luck was truly on the side of true love. Using his paw, Bentley slowly opened the bedroom door, and we both entered the room.

"Bentley? What are you doing here?" a sweet little voice asked, and my heart melted upon hearing it.

"Lexi, I came to check on you and introduce you to a new friend of mine. Come in, Wallace."

I emerged from behind Bentley, feeling shy as I felt both pair of eyes on me. Papa had just taken Bentley and me to our favorite groomer: Puppy Pet Spa. We had our matching spiked collars and Hawaiian flower pattern bandanas that matched the summer vibe. We also had our signature puppy cuts which were not too short, not too long.

"Hello," I tried to say, but nothing came out.

"Lexi, this is Wallace, Wallace, this is Lexi," Bentley spoke up, seeing how I had frozen.

I was awestruck. It was like time had stopped, and Lexi and my eyes met. I was in love here, and gazing at me was the most beautiful creature I had ever seen in my life.

"Hello, Wallace," she said softly and pulled her hair away, decorated with two beautiful pink bows.

From there, it was a blur. Lexi and I started meeting secretly without Papa, Mama, and Grandma noticing. Bentley would cover for us and place snoopy dolls in my place. Surprisingly no one noticed. I even think Papa sat petting the stuffed decoy dog once on the couch. Bentley sat in his bed laughing. Whenever Mama or Papa would look for me, Bentley would knock the trash over or steal Papa's shoe having him chase him down the hallway.

Meanwhile, Lexi and I had the time of our lives. Papa and Mama would have their date nights while we had date nights of our own. We would sneak out to go disco dancing at happy hour for treats and drinks, always remembering to bring some back for Bentley. He was happy to have Lexi off his back. What's one dog's trash is another dog's treasure, as they say. But then again, since things were going too well, they were bound to go downhill pretty soon.

Bentley and I also loved to watch WWF wrestling with Papa, along with his friends. Mama meanwhile had started a Tough Readers book club. While Mama and Papa went to work everyday, me and Bentley would wait for them and get into trouble sometimes taking our wrestling reenactments too far. Bentley and Papa really loved the attitude era so I would play along as the Rock, Bentley as Stone Cold Steve Austin. Mainly I just loved singing, trash talking and doing the peoples elbow to Bentley. He would take Papa's beer out the fridge and go crazy. It was fun times until mama found us and had to take us to the emergency vet.

One of Papa's friends, whom everyone called Head, owing to his obviously large head, always told us that he would become a famous wrestler someday, and we all laughed at him. But the joke was on us, as years later, he became a famous wrestler and changed his name to Che Cabrera. He was really happy when Mama's future social service client became his fan.

Bentley and I at night had to adjust to our weird sleeping patterns with Mama and Papa under the covers with me sleeping between them, resting my head on the pillow and snuggled under the blanket. Bentley loved to sleep on Mama and Papa's legs and bite them in their sleep if they moved. One night, Papa got a bleeding toe, but Bentley was safe. I was surprised that they never got mad at him. That dog could definitely get away with murder and still be regarded as a saint. Bentley also had this habit of pretending that he was hurt just for attention. He would jump off the bed and pretend that his paw got injured. He would walk around limping and crying all day long. It didn't just end there, Mama and Papa would take him to the vet, and I would get so mad at him.

"You stupid, phony poodle! You have been troubling Mama and Papa with the vets and groomers. They spend thousands of dollars on your antics, and it is not fair!" I would often yell at him whenever he would get his paw stuck in a blanket or get dirt all over him. Bentley loved to brag about how much Mama and Papa would spend and max out their credit cards on him. It was so ridiculous.

It was also because I was a tough and manly dog, I couldn't deal with his drama and clumsiness, but he also managed to make me laugh at times. He also had this silly dance in which he would stand on his hind legs and beg at the table, swooshing his paws, for treats. It worked like a charm all the time. On the other hand, I was gifted with a beautiful singing voice. I sang along all the time to Papa's tunes on the guitar. I also became famous ever since Mama started uploading my singing videos on YouTube.

I loved Mama the most, I loved to sit on her lap, and whenever we went shopping, I would sit with Mama in her driving seat and pretend to drive the car. Bentley and my bond grew over time while getting matching haircuts at the groomers, snuggling on our dog beds like loving brothers, and Bentley would read to me at night to help me fall asleep from time to time.

One day, while Lexi and I had snuck out to go on a small stroll, Grandma came to check on her and saw the stuffed dog animal in her cage. She instantly panicked, thinking that someone had snuck inside her apartment and stolen Lexi. We weren't too far from the apartments and heard the commotion.

"Oh no!" Lexi instantly recognized her owner's voice and rushed upstairs.

I didn't think things through as I followed her, and much to my horror, that was how Grandma saw us coming in together.

"Wallace? What have you done to my poor Lexi? Like father like a dog!" she shrieked and kicked me in the process of picking up Lexi and hugging her close to her body.

"What the hell!" I yelped in pain at the impact.

I ran back to my apartment, scared and startled, upon feeling the sharp pain that ran through my body. As I reached the apartment, I saw Mama, and I ran up to her, scratching her leg so she would pick me up.

"What's wrong, my baby? Are you okay? What happened?" Mama asked, worried about me.

She picked me up and tried to calm me down, but it was to no avail. More than my body, my heart hurt knowing that the jig was up. Now that Grandma knew about my love for Lexi, she would never let us meet again, locking the door and whatnot. I whimpered in Mama's arms in pain at the thought of not seeing Lexi again. She would no longer trust Lexi to be left alone either, which would simply mean more time in a locked cage.

"Oh, my poor Lexi..." I whimpered in sadness.

I lay beside Bentley and cried all night as he comforted me. I didn't know when I was going to see the love of my life again, and the days started to feel longer, almost as if they would never end. One day, when it had been a week since I had seen Lexi, it surprised me suddenly. I remember every tiny detail clearly as the day. Papa was taking the family to a car show for his 1969 Mustang, and nobody was home except Bentley and I.

"Oh, I hope she doesn't lock her door..." I prayed.

As soon as everyone left, I quickly went outside the apartment but much to my dismay; the screendoor was locked.

"Lexi!" I called out to her, hoping she wasn't locked inside her cage.

Much to my happiness, I heard pitter-patter, the sound of Lexi's small feet hitting the tiled floor as she ran toward me. My heart took a leap in my chest, excited to see her after the longest week of my life.

"How have you been, my love? I missed you so much!" I screamed out as soon as I saw her, beautiful as ever.

"Wallace! Oh, how I missed you so!" she responded from the other side of the screen door, which I wanted to tear apart for separating us, but I knew Evil Grandma would never let Mama or Papa hear the end of it.

"You have no idea how much I missed you! Poor Bentley never heard the end of it..."

"I have some news for you, Wallace!" Lexi suddenly spoke shyly.

"What happened?" I asked, hoping she would be okay.

"You are going to be a father, Wallace!" she told me, and my heart soared with happiness upon the news.

"BENTLEY! IM GOING TO BE A FATHER!" I yelled in glee, prancing around the front door. Bentley, lying on the other side of the door, smiled at us.

"Congratulations to both of you! Looks like I'll be a godfather faster than I thought I'd be!" we laughed at the comment. I loved him so much.

Soon enough, everyone found out about Lexi and my babies. Grandma, of course, was furious. Mama and Papa were beyond happy for us, which is all that mattered at the end for me. Time went by much faster from there onwards, and soon Lexi gave birth to two healthy puppies.

"This one is Paris, and this one is London!" I heard Mama say to Grandma as we all sat around the babies and Lexi. I thought Grandma would reject the names, but not only did she accept them, I could swear I saw a small smile on her face. Grandma kept my babies with her and Lexi, but as they grew and moved around, Grandma would bring them over. They loved Mama very much and would run all over our apartment. Watching them, I realized that I was so happy and proud. From a starving street dog, I now had a family, a beautiful wife, Mama, Papa, along my best friend And brother Bentley.

I was beyond happy.

Chapter 3: The Wedding, Bentley and Wallace Saves the Day

My life had been rather hectic ever since I became a father. Paris and London were quite the handful, always running around and disturbing Lexi while she slept. I had always heard that it was a huge blessing to become a father, but some nights were too frustrating for me to be grateful for the two little active pups who had just learned to bark. They would play, fall, trip, and yowl because of the pain until Mama would come and pick them up and coddle them. Don't get me wrong, I loved them both to no end and would even die for them, but some days I would miss the peace and quiet.

That being said, I found out Bentley had a staggering amount of patience, fit to be a godfather. Paris and London would nibble on his ears and tumble on his feet while he was sleeping, and Bentley wouldn't even move. He would often sneak them small treats and play with them too, which was a rather odd sight. What was even odder was that some days I would catch Grandma passing a smile, too, watching the pups play. I'm pretty sure she didn't approve of our relationship still, but she had become more lenient in the sense of letting me see my wife and kids.

Mama and Papa called London and Paris their grandkids, and I would love to hear it, but Grandma would always intervene.

"How can you have any grandkids when you aren't even married?" she would comment, and Mama's face would visibly grow sad.

"We will get married soon..." she would reply softly, but her words lacked any sense of belief in them.

"Sure, you will..."

Mama would constantly push Papa to marry her already, and for some reason or another, Papa kept delaying the whole ordeal. He would make foolish excuses, which would make Mama angrier.

No matter how much Mama would assure him that money was never an issue for her, Papa would simply shake his head and walk away. I understood Papa's struggles to an extent, though. I also wanted to give Lexi, London, and Paris the whole world if I could, but then again, that never stopped me from marrying Lexi. I hoped Papa would hurry and marry Mama as they were practically married anyway.

You see, Mama was always full of determination. When she wanted something, she made sure it happened, and this time, she wanted to marry Papa. He was a bit hesitant at first, but Mama was adamant and didn't take no for an answer. She even bought a wedding ring to show how serious she was. When Papa said no again, Mama got angry and returned the ring. But she wasn't the one to back down!

On her birthday, Mama was back with another plan. She decided that they had to get married, and this time, she wasn't going to listen to Papa's objections. She picked out another ring, this time from JCPenney. It was not that expensive, but again Mama had never been interested in money anyway. She planned a lovely getaway to Santa Barbara for the four of us- Bentley, Mama, Papa, and me. They would usually go there on weekends and often took us along. We loved going on trips, especially when there was wine tasting, something Mama loved. Mama and Papa decided to get our auras read, and I must say, boy! It was a fascinating experience. Mama even managed to snap a photo of the three of us, and I had to sneak a paw in the shot. Mama shared the photo on Facebook, and we had finally become an official and happy family, our friends were thrilled about the news too.

But there was a bit of a hitch in our wedding plans. Mama's friend, Laura, who was really rude to her, decided to have her wedding before ours and even used some of the same girls Mama wanted in her wedding party. That didn't sit well with Mama, especially when Laura scheduled her wedding just three months before ours. Even Grandma and Papa picked most of the family and friends without much of Mama's opinion. However, Mama still went ahead with the dreamy and big wedding that she had planned. She found an old beautiful ranch to have the wedding and also got outfits for Bentley and me. But overall Mama didn't care, it was a fun year with four big weddings of their friend group.

"You two look dashing!" Mama cooed as we tried on our dresses.

Papa smirked, "Well, they couldn't let me be the only handsome one on this special day, right?"

However, we were disappointed and heartbroken after learning that Bentley and I were not invited to the wedding! Grandma refused to include us. It was absolutely outrageous! We had been practicing our walk down the aisle, and Bentley had even prepared a speech. She was a traditional soul, and in her eyes, weddings were strictly human affairs. She didn't quite understand our deep bond with Mama and Papa and thought we should stay out of their big day. But Bentley and I were determined to show Grandma that our love for Mama and Papa was just as strong as any human's love. We knew in our hearts that we were part of their family, and we couldn't imagine missing such an important event in their lives. So, in the days leading up to the wedding, we made sure to put on our most adorable expressions whenever we were around Grandma. We'd give her those "puppy eyes" that no one can resist, hoping she'd change her mind. We'd follow her around, wagging our tails and showering her with affection to win her over.

But despite all our efforts, Grandma remained firm. She would shake her head and say, "No, no, dogs don't belong in weddings. It's just not proper."

Something really upsetting also happened the night before the wedding, which hurt Mama a lot. Papa and Mama had a baseless argument, and Papa called the whole wedding a sham. But they went on with the wedding anyway.

Bentley and I did not sit around and mope. We decided to take matters into our own paws. We knew Papa was planning to use his vintage 1969 Mustang in the wedding for photos and their grand exit, so we hatched a plan. We hid in the back of the Mustang under some blankets, ready to surprise Mama and Papa.

However, things didn't go exactly as we planned. Papa had the key to the car, and we had to use another way to get inside. As we snuck into the old house, we could already hear the ceremony starting.

We trotted in through the old kitchen door; everyone was getting ready for the event. We snuck past the crew and saw the bridal rooms where Mama and Papa were getting ready. Everyone was happy, and most of them were already drunk. We went to the backdoor, where all the preparations were made, and hid.

The venue was a dream! It was an old charming ranch in the heart of the countryside, surrounded by big hills and trees. The ranch had a rustic charm. Wooden signs pointed the way, adorned with elegant calligraphy, guiding everyone to the ceremony site. The pathway leading to the ceremony was lined with wildflowers, creating a whimsical and romantic ambiance. The ceremony was set up under a majestic oak tree, its sprawling branches providing natural shade. Rustic wooden benches were arranged in a semi-circle, facing a simple wooden arch adorned with red and blue flowers, which was the theme of the wedding. It was a sight to behold, and the love in the air was palpable. There were almost a hundred people in the area.

The ceremony was about to begin, and Bentley and I were anxious, hiding in the bushes, waiting for our moment to surprise Mama and Papa. As the harpist began to play, everyone stood in anticipation. Mama looked absolutely radiant in her flowing white gown, a touch of red and blue in her bouquet, while Papa stood proudly by her side in a dashing black suit with a red tie to match the theme. Mama looked stunning, and Papa couldn't take his eyes off her.

As soon as Mama was about to walk down the aisle, we couldn't contain our excitement and jumped right into her arms! People, especially Grandma, were shocked to see us, Mama cried in happiness, but Papa couldn't stop laughing, and that's what mattered most. She carried us to the altar, where Mama and Papa exchanged vows that they had written themselves, promising to love, cherish and support each other through thick and thin. Mama and Papa were pronounced as husband and wife; the guests erupted into applause. It was official - our little family was now officially united.

The reception area was equally charming and beautifully decorated in red and blue accents. Long wooden tables were draped with rustic burlap runners and adorned with mason jars filled with wildflowers. The centerpiece of each table featured a small wooden figurine of Mama, Papa, Bentley, and me, and the cake toppers were replicas of us, too, sitting on top of a delightful three-tiered cake decorated with red and blue flowers.

The food was a delicious array of farm-to-table delights, served family-style to encourage guests to bond and share in the joy of the celebration. Laughter filled the air as friends and family raised their glasses in toasts to Mama and Papa's love. Bentley and I had the time of our lives, too, running around, stealing cuddles and belly rubs from everyone, and joining in the fun whenever someone threw a frisbee or a ball our way.

As the sun began to set, the atmosphere turned magical. String lights twinkled overhead, casting a warm glow across the dance floor. Mama and Papa shared their first dance together as a married couple, holding each other close, and Bentley and I watched with wagging tails from the sidelines.

Later that night, the reception was a blast. There was a DJ on the floor, and throughout the evening, the dance floor came alive with vibrant energy as guests kicked off their shoes and danced the night away. "You boys are the life of the party!" Ashley said, laughing and patting our heads.

"Look, Wallace and Bentley are stealing the show!" someone exclaimed.

Papa was grinning from ear to ear. "I always knew they were the stars of the family," he said proudly.

“LEXI,” both Bentley and I exclaimed in happiness as she snuck out of the Mustang with her girls, wearing matching dresses. "Wallace and Bentley, you two are quite the troublemakers," Lexi said, shaking her head playfully.

"We couldn't let Mama and Papa get married without us!" Bentley replied, wagging his tail.

"I forgive you two, but crashing a wedding is a bit audacious," Lexi said, laughing.

"We couldn't have imagined this day without them," Mama replied, looking fondly at us.

Papa added, "They're part of our family, and today is about all of us being together."

Our determination to be there for Mama and Papa had won everyone's hearts. And looking back, crashing the wedding turned out to be one of the most heartwarming and memorable experiences of our doggy lives. We proved that love knows no bounds and that a dog's loyalty and devotion are as real and significant as anyone else's. The celebration went on late into the night, and we all had the time of our lives. Mama and Papa were glowing with happiness, surrounded by their loved ones. Bentley, Papa, and I had a little jam session as we gathered in the house after the wedding. Papa played his guitar, Bentley hit the piano keys, and I barked in rhythm. It was a beautiful moment, and everyone joined in the fun.

The next day, Mama and Papa left for their honeymoon in Cabo, but our bond as a family grew even stronger. In the end, our wedding might have been unconventional, but it was perfect for us. Mama's determination and love brought us all together, and Bentley and I couldn't have been happier to be part of such a special day. It was a day of love, laughter, and a celebration of family, and I'm grateful that I got to be there to witness it all.

Chapter 4: Papa Gets Promoted, The De La Os find a new home in San Luis Obispo

Bentley and I were wrestling as usual, laughing, prancing around, and jumping on each other. Our barks resonated around the house as Mama watched us and laughed at how stupid we probably looked with our antics. However, it was so much fun that we insisted on doing it every day. After we healed from our emergency visit, we decided to tone down the extreme matches. It had become routine for us. Bentley and my bond grew stronger with time and I stopped thinking of him as a poodle with poor decision-making skills and a chaotic spirit. In fact, I had quite started to like his chaos because it kept me entertained.

As Mama sipped on her tea there was a sound of a key being put in the lock on the front door. "I'm home!" Papa called out. He rushed into the living room in a flurry and Bentley and I stopped our game and looked at him intently with our heads tilting to the side in unison.

"I have some news, Ashley!" Roy exclaimed.

"What happened?" asked Mama. "Wait, is it good or bad?" she paused with her eyes widening.

"It's great, Ash! I have finally been promoted to Assistant Manager. "Ah, all that effort did finally pay off!"

This was a great achievement because of how bad the corporate system is and how their employees' efforts go unappreciated. 'This is huge news,' I thought to myself. 'All those years of struggle.'

Just seeing him like that made me smile.

Papa originally got the job when he was 18 with Demon Brent. He was assigned to pick up trash as a janitor. Brent was fired from pretending to get carts while hanging out at the mall. Mama on the other hand, after college tried subbing but she felt she was too smart to be teaching kids all day.

Mama was utterly exhausted after her marriage to Papa. The whirlwind of wedding preparations, the emotional rollercoaster, and the excitement of starting a new life had taken its toll on her. She longed for a peaceful break, a chance to catch her breath and rejuvenate her spirit. With a sigh of relief, she looked forward to some quiet moments to reflect on her journey so far, and perhaps plan for the future with Papa. As she sat down in the cozy corner of their new home, she felt grateful for the love and support she had received throughout the festivities, but now, she cherished the idea of a moment of solitude to unwind and recharge.

The only friends who didn't get married were Uncle Ronnie and Aunt Carol who were pretty hurt that he didn't propose. Since Ronnie and Carol lived at Auntie Nora's building two doors down she didn't have to witness the fights and abuse that would take place between them but she heard stories from her sister which also didn't sit well with Mama. Carol often would cry at our apartment telling horrors of her adopted family and foster home experiences. She later moved out of the valley to Chinatown often updating Mama on her adventures. Mamas other friend Jenny our dog sitter was in their wedding but was dating an abusive guy as well during this time, Mama often consoling her along with their other book club co-founder Cindy who lived in a condo down the street. She and her partner also didn't marry but later sold their condo in Chatsworth to buy a home together. Mama was happy when their book club participant Amanda later had a beautiful Gothic wedding at the same ranch on Halloween with black and purple colors and horror movie themed tables. Mama, Jenny and Papa along with their book club sat at the Beetlejuice table, taking home the book gifts "Never Trust the Living."

Mama was kind to people but I observed that she didn't seem to be very good at forming close friendships or had an unwillingness towards it often quoting Kurt Cobain, "A friend is a known enemy" as she helped make the males in their group Nirvana cover band flyers to pass out for their local bar shows. Unlike the strong bond I share with Bentley and Lexi, it appeared that Mama and the other humans around her struggled to understand how to be good friends with each other. They communicated in ways that were quite different from our canine language, with the women barking at each other and the men engaging in petty behaviors. As a dog, I always felt lucky to have such loyal and loving companions in Bentley and Lexi, and I couldn't quite comprehend the complexities of human relationships. But through it all, I remained grateful for the unconditional love and companionship I received from my dear doggy friends.

From a dog's perspective, Mama seemed really happy and excited about her Marketing job working for an old Demon Brent drummer man during these days who would tell stories when he played with the Grateful Dead and his business partner Dolly. They were kind and caring towards Mama and Papa, which made the whole experience enjoyable for our family. They even sent them to San Francisco for a Chinese New Year's event, which must have been a fantastic adventure!

However, after three years, Mama felt like she needed a change and decided to explore the big ad agency world. She joined Time Warner media in Brentwood, where people seemed to be having a lot of fun, sometimes acting like characters from the popular TV show Mad Men. Mama loved making her coworkers laugh, and it seemed like a cheerful and vibrant atmosphere.

Papa was happy too because they received free tickets to events at the Staple Center, and they even got to see Lady Gaga perform once in their fancy company booth! Mama and Papa also enjoyed sharing their experiences with friends, taking Mama's best friend Aunt Cammie to a Clipper game together.

As a dog, I couldn't fully grasp the details of Mama's work life, but I could sense that she cherished her time with both companies and appreciated the opportunities they brought to our family. She seemed to be a source of joy and laughter for everyone around her.

It was a journey of ups and downs, but Mama found her calling at PathaPoint, a social services non-profit. She had started working there after a creepy Christian ad agency fired her for being a "heathen" as they called her. She found Pathapoint online and decided she wanted to help people. Also, it wasn't too far from their house as Mama was still traumatized from the car accident Papa had to save her from while working at Time Warner Media. Only three months into the Pathapoint job she was very well liked.

Mama came home shortly after with a surprise cake for Papa. "Guess what? PathPoint is letting me transfer to their Residential Department in San Luis Obispo, they are so nice!"

With excitement and a hint of sadness, our family packed our belongings and bid farewell to our old home. As we drove through the scenic countryside, Mama explained to us how this move was an adventure full of new opportunities. She had this twinkle in her eye that was priceless. I loved both my parents and always wanted to see them happy.

Mama found a cheap apartment next to a creepy mental hospital in Atascadero's little town. Bentley and I were not very pleased at the thought of living there. What if the mental hospital was haunted and we all got possessed by demons?

Auntie Nora made the decision to put Mama in a mental hospital after she graduated college. This might have been influenced by Mama and Cammie's drinking and partying lifestyle at that time. Mama hated subbing, she often felt like Paris and Nicole Richie from The Simple Life going to very conservative private schools with a company called Teachers on Reserve.

Fast Forward since then, it appeared that Mama had become somewhat obsessed with mental hospitals, possibly due to her personal experience or the lingering effects of being in one. This newfound interest might be rooted in trying to understand her own past and experiences. She felt conflicted that a lot were closing down as she often felt it was nice to have a sanctuary away from the world and safety.

Speaking of demons, the apartment manager came to the home the next day to have a meeting with Mama. I did not like her vibe at all.

"Hey, Bentley," I spoke up one day as I basked in the sun rays streaming in from the bedroom window. "Do you think the apartment manager is a little creepy?"

Bentley was lying on his back with his paws spread out. "I don't like her at all," he said.

"Right?! I knew I wasn't the only one!"

The following day, Mama took us on a tour of the town, showing us the art galleries, bookstores, and parks. We discovered a lively farmer's market filled with colorful stalls selling fresh produce and artisanal goods. The aroma of freshly baked bread and the sound of music filled the air, making the experience magical.

We were finally settling into our new home. We had come a long way since their move to San Luis Obispo, and each member had found their place in the town.

Whenever the apartment manager came around, Bentley and I would start growling at her.

"Stayyy," Mama scolded us one day. Then she turned to the demon manager. "Sorry, I don't know what's gotten into them."

Disregarding Mama's orders, I jumped at the evil manager and started to bite her shins, with Bentley following my lead. We barked and circled the woman, still trying to nip at her feet. The idiot screamed and jumped up on the living room couch. 'Freaking coward,' I thought to myself.

"HEY!" Mama screamed at the top of her lungs. "STOP IT YOU TWO!"

Bentley and I stopped dead in our tracks. We put our tails between our legs and exited the living room.

"Boy, have we messed up," said Bentley.

The mailman would come from time to time and I would bark loudly at him from behind the screen door. He would drop whatever packages he had for Mama and Papa and rush to get out of my vicinity. Finally, I knew how to fend for my family. The mailman wouldn't ever imagine hurting us. I hated the guy.

Bentley and I started playing our instruments all day listening to the bells of the hospital. We started our own band like Papa and his friends. Bentley played drums, and I sang and played guitar. We would play covers of "Institutionalized and Hotel California." Bentley would be on vocals "I just wanted a Pepsi," he would jokingly sing. Although we were having fun, the manager was not pleased. He'd call Mama and Papa while they were at work.

"Your dogs are playing and singing again pissing off the neighbors!" he would complain. Compared to evil Grandma she was very strict. I started to miss Grandma actually and made me appreciate her.

The next day, Mama went out and returned with special collars that would shock us every time we messed up. I thought it was so unfair. I had a duty. And that was to protect my parents and my brother.

I was so upset, my voice was being taken away from me. Who was I if I could not bark or protect our home?

I noticed that Mama had been acting differently lately too. She seemed eager and excited, trying various strange potions and attending regular acupuncture. I observed her dedication to getting pregnant, as she spent a lot of time researching and talking to others about it.

I became more attentive to her needs. I noticed when she was feeling down or stressed and tried to offer comfort with my presence and affection. I sensed her joy when she received positive news or support, and I could also feel her disappointment when things didn't go as planned.

Throughout the process, I remained by her side, providing unwavering love and companionship. I may have not fully understood what she was going through, but I sensed the importance of her quest to become a parent, and I became an empathetic and caring presence throughout the journey.

One day, Mama walked into the bedroom where Papa was playing with me. He would throw my favorite plush toy across the room and I was to fetch it for him. I was having such great fun.

"I have news for you!" she exclaimed. "You're going to be a father!" she said to Papa.

Papa looked confused for a second. He kept looking at Mama with wide eyes. Then the realization hit him. "Wait, what?! For real?!" he screamed.

He got up from the bed and gave Mama a long, harsh kiss. He picked her up and swung her around in his arms. "I can't believe this!"

"Better believe it, Dad," Mama teased him.

Bentley had heard the commotion and had walked inside the room, his tail shaking a mile a minute. He had heard everything. He excitedly started to circle Mama's feet and licked her toes with affection.

"Aww, my sweet boy!" said Mama. She picked him up and hugged him close.

The news of Mama being pregnant spread quickly, and we were overjoyed. Many friends and relatives visited them to share their excitement and offer their love and support.

As Thanksgiving approached, our family had another reason to celebrate our new house and the new addition to the family that was about to arrive.

On Thanksgiving Day, the house was buzzing with activity. Even Grandpa Stuart flew in. I hadn't seen him in so long. Another time Evil Grandma came up with more cousins and took them to get some famous ice cream downtown. Other friends showed up like Cammie, Uncle Ronnie now dating Jenny's best friend whom Papa had a crush on, and Demon Brent's family. Laura after the wedding had a boy. Mama was happy for her but she also gave Mama a hard time for not being there when she had something called post-traumatic stress syndrome causing more tension to their friendship. Mama later nicknamed her Cammie 2.0 as they made similar petty remarks.

Finally, time was passing more quickly it seemed when Mama's belly was getting bigger and the holidays were approaching. Thanksgiving day, the aroma of a delicious feast filled the air, as Mama and Papa worked together in the kitchen, preparing a mouthwatering turkey and a variety of delectable side dishes. The excitement was palpable as they looked forward to sharing this special meal with their loved ones.

As the guests arrived, the house became even livelier. Laughter and chatter filled every room, and the warmth of love and togetherness enveloped everyone. The dining table was adorned with autumn-themed decorations, and the family gathered around it, holding hands to say a heartfelt prayer of gratitude before indulging in the lavish meal.

During dinner, stories and memories were shared, and everyone took turns expressing what they were thankful for. From cherished moments with family and friends to personal achievements and the anticipation of the new baby's arrival, the atmosphere was filled with gratitude and joy.

After the meal, some guests went outside to play games and enjoy the crisp autumn weather. Bentley and my parents took a moment to reflect on the journey that led them to this new house and expressed their gratitude for the blessings they had received.

As the evening progressed, desserts were served, and the family enjoyed a variety of sweet treats. The kids ran around with their cousins, laughing and playing, while the adults sat together, content in each other's company.

As the night came to a close, the family bid their farewells to their loved ones, thanking them for being a part of such a memorable Thanksgiving celebration. The new house had indeed become a symbol of love, growth, and togetherness for our family.

The next few months were filled with anticipation and excitement as we prepared for the new addition to our family. Through it all, the memories of that Thanksgiving in the new house remained etched in our hearts, reminding us of the blessings we were grateful for and the love that surrounded us.

Meanwhile, the hurt from Papa's words made Mama's dedication to her clients a way of coping and was also evident as she diligently handled her reports and case notes from the comfort of her home. It allowed her to balance her responsibilities as a soon-to-be mother and a compassionate professional. The positive impact she made on her clients' lives was heartwarming, and it even led to a kind gesture from one of her clients who bought us a dog holder for her car, making outings more enjoyable for Bentley and me.

I noticed Mama and Papa were arguing more often and the atmosphere in the house had gotten tense. I heard Papa yell once, "I came up here for my career, what are you going to do? Stay here or go back to your mom's?" Mama was heartbroken. I wondered what was happening to our happy family where no one disagreed and everyone lived in harmony despite their differences. This was new territory for me and Bentley. We tried to lighten the mood most times by cuddling up to Mama and Papa and trying to play with them. They would cheer up for a while but go back to being sulky.

"Wallace, what's happening to Mama and Papa? Why are they fighting?" asked Bentley one day.

"It's cause Papa is a piece of poop."

I laughed, he knew there was nothing that could be done because Mama and Papa were so set in their own ways.

At night, Bentley, in an attempt to get attention from Mama, would jump on her bed and wake her up at 3 a.m.

"She needs her sleep, you idiot!" I scolded Bentley. "Even I'm trying to sleep here!"

"Oh, suck it up!" said Bentley, sniffling at me.

'What the heck do I do with him?' I wonder.

"You stupid Demon dog!" I would curse at him. "Doing your demon things in the middle of the night, disturbing the peace! You degenerate poodle!" I growled at him once but he never listened.

One night, I really wanted to get some sleep because we were supposed to participate in a dog costume competition and I needed my beauty sleep for it so I could look fresh and alert during the show. However, the chaos ensued at 3 am as usual.

When morning came, Mama dressed me and Bentley smartly and took us in the car to the competition.

The dog costume competition was initially an exciting event where Bentley and I showcased our best costumes. We were eager to impress the judges and the audience with our cuteness and best behavior. However, as the competition progressed, I noticed some unfair advantages being given to certain participants. It became apparent that some dogs were favored over others, and the judging process seemed biased.

As the competition neared its end, I discovered that some dogs had received insider information about the judges' preferences, giving them an unfair advantage. This information was leaked by someone close to the organizing team, leading to a rigged outcome.

Despite their best efforts, Bentley and I didn't stand a chance against the dogs with the inside knowledge, and the results left us feeling disappointed and disheartened. Even Mama looked bummed at the fact that we had lost. She had put a lot of effort into our costumes, only to realize that the competition wasn't on a level playing field.

Now, Bentley and I were left with a sense of betrayal and frustration, knowing that our hard work was overshadowed by unfair practices in the competition. We hoped that future events would be conducted with integrity and transparency to ensure a fair and enjoyable experience for all participants. However, we headed back home with our heads hanging down.

One day, my world turned upside down. I walked into the living room with Mama holding Bentley close to her as tears streamed down her face. The atmosphere of the room was somber. I was alarmed.

'Why is Mama crying?' I thought to myself, concerned.

"Bentley?" I said out loud but he didn't say anything. He turned to look at me.

"Oh, Wallace. I am so sorry," he said, his voice cracking.

"What? What happened?" I was confused.

"It's Lexi," Bentley gasped. "She passed away."

The room started spinning. "What are you saying?" I laughed. I thought he was joking. Then as I watched Mama and Bentley for a few moments, I realized what he was actually trying to tell me.

“No,” I barked. “This cannot be possible! Is this some sort of sick joke?”

“No. she had sudden kidney failure,” replied Bentley.

My heart was shattered into a million pieces. My companion. The love of my life. Was gone in an instant.

Weeks went by and I refused to have any food. I would stay in my doggy bed with my face buried in it. Mama and Papa were concerned for me.

“Looks like he’s sensed the loss of Lexi,” said Mama. “Oh, you poor thing,” she said as she lifted me out of my bed and held me close to her heart. I welcomed her tender embrace and tears started falling from my eyes. I whined against her chest as she stroked my fur.

I was a playful and energetic pup who loved running around in the lakes with Bentley. I felt so happy when Mama was around, as her joy was contagious and made our playtime even more delightful. However, after the loss of Lexi, I lost interest in everything.

As time passed and we had to move back to the Valley, I noticed a change in Mama's demeanor. She seemed sad and distant, which made me concerned. I could sense the tension between Mama and Papa, and it affected the entire household. I missed the carefree days by the lakes, and longed for Mama's cheerful presence to return, bringing back the happiness and playfulness we once shared together.

Mama started feeling uncomfortable at Papa's Home Depot parties as a result of Papa's hurtful words and behavior.

Despite enjoying her work, Mama kept to herself, indicating that she found solace and fulfillment in her professional life rather than seeking closeness within the family circle. I noticed she started to build an emotional wall against Papa.

Papa's actions went down a troubling path. He became friends with a manager who was cheating on his wife, which only added more tension to their already strained relationship. Mama was uncomfortable with this situation and refused to be around the manager's wife, leading to further arguments with Papa.

To make matters worse, Papa's behavior at his job also became inappropriate with female colleagues, causing even more distress for Mama. Although she refrained from saying "I told you so," she couldn't help but feel disappointed and unsurprised by the consequences of Papa's choices.

Eventually, the situation reached a breaking point, and we had to move back to the valley. Papa was somewhat relieved to be reunited with his old friends, but the underlying issues in their relationship remained unresolved. The toxic dynamics between them continued to strain their marriage, leaving Mama in a difficult position, trying to balance her career, desire for motherhood, and the emotional challenges caused by Papa's attitude.

Chapter 5: Back to the Valley; Charlotte Is Born

Time flew by, and Bentley and I were sullen over the tension between Mama and Papa. This was supposed to be a joyous time because of the arrival of their child.

One day, Mama went to the hospital and came back with a huge smile on her face. "Hey guys!" she said as she walked into the house. Her energy was contagious, and it already had Bentley and me shaking our tails as we sat at her feet with big smiles on our faces.

'I wonder why she's so happy,' I wondered what it was that could have possibly made her this happy. It had been a long time since we saw her beaming like that.

Mama got down on her knees and planted a kiss on Bentley and my snouts. "Guess what, my babies! I'm going to be a mother to a baby girl!"

My ears perked up. 'Oh my goodness,' I thought to myself. "I'm going to have a sister!"

Bentley and I started dancing at Mama's feet, invoking laughter from her. She was positively glowing, and we basked in the light of her happiness.

I couldn't wait. Bentley and I waited impatiently.

"Gosh, a baby sister," said Bentley one day. "We're going to have so much fun with her. She will be our new friend!"

"Yes, we will be the best of friends!" I replied.

Time passed by painfully slow since we got the news. Finally, Mama was nine months along, and we were as excited as ever. We even caught Papa smiling to himself as he zoned out while watching TV.

As the due date approached, Mama's belly swelled with the promise of new life, and we could feel the anticipation building in the household. Bentley and I became extra vigilant, making sure to stay close to Mama, and offering comfort and companionship as she navigated the last stages of her pregnancy.

Before she had the baby, Mama, and Papa tried to move back to our old cheap apartment. They went to speak to Grandma about it. However, they returned with disappointment on their faces. They found out that Grandma had given the apartment to Mama's nephew Keanu. He had apparently been living there for a long time. 'Well, no way to get rid of him now,' I thought to myself.

To make matters worse, his entire family was living there. How could we displace them? I was kind of angry at Grandma for doing this to us. 'Maybe I should bark at her the next time she comes around,' I thought to myself. Mama's older brother Uncle Cole scolded them that they couldn't take it back.

In the end, we only had one option, and that was to move into Grandpa Wade's house, which was also Papa's old house. The house was absolutely disgusting and was in shambles. It seemed like no one had ever cleaned the house. The paint was chipping, revealing the grey walls underneath; it was really ugly. The floorboards creaked as you walked over them. They were uprooted from the corners. There was dust everywhere, and it made Papa sneeze a lot. They knew they had to do something to improve our residence in the house. Needless to say, we missed our previous house.

This house was not at all up to the standards of me Bentley, and Mama. However, we didn't have a choice, and Grandpa Wade was kind enough to give us a place to stay, so I couldn't really complain. Beggars can't be choosers, right?

"We should renovate this dump," said Papa to Mama one day, who agreed.

As a result, they pooled money to renovate the house just to make it more livable and less miserable looking. Before the changes, it looked as if a troll lived there. Hence, they painted the house and put in new wooden flooring to get the house up to par. Mama updated Aunt Evelyn's old room for our baby sister.

As the days passed, Mama's excitement for the impending arrival of her baby girl only grew stronger. She spent time decorating the nursery with gray, pink, and white, carefully choosing toys and clothes for her little bundle of joy. Bentley and I eagerly watched her preparations, excited to meet our new sibling.

Throughout Mama's pregnancy, Papa seemed distant and preoccupied, still carrying the weight of the tension that had been lingering between them. However, Mama's unwavering happiness and optimism slowly started to influence him too. He began to participate in the preparations, helping Mama set up the crib and painting the walls with her. It was all very cute.

We observed everything that was going on in the house to make sure all operations were running smoothly. Bentley and I would run in circles around the house as we, too, could feel the palpable excitement.

Now Grandpa Wade was a rude old man who picked fights with everyone. He had a problem with everything. "Why are you spending so much money for stupid crap?" he asked one day.

'What a dumb question.' I thought to myself. 'The old man has lost his marbles.'

He would fight with Mama for no reason and say mean things to her. At first, she tried her best to ignore him, but the leech never seemed to stop. It was as if he was finding new reasons to ridicule Mama. This broke my heart. She was so sweet and so fragile in her state; I never understood how someone could be so rude to her. There were many times when I saw her sitting on the driver's side of the car outside and crying. I looked out of the window in concern. I wanted to go out and comfort her, but the screen door was shut. I wished I had learned how to open it like Bentley. He was the clever one when it came to this stuff. They had yet to install the doggy door.

Despite their moments of happiness, the ongoing feuds between Papa and Mama continue to cast a shadow over their relationship. The back-and-forth exchanges seemed to provide a fleeting sense of excitement, a temporary distraction from their underlying issues. However, as time passed, it became increasingly clear that these conflicts were taking a toll on their bond.

While both Papa and Mama might have managed to find joy in their shared moments, Mama's resentment towards Papa's behavior lingered. The hurtful words exchanged during their arguments left scars that never healed to this day. Mama's patience wore thin, and she found it difficult to overlook the patterns of behavior that had been the root cause of their disagreements.

The emotional distance between them gradually grew wider. Their interactions, once filled with warmth and companionship, were now marked by tension and strained politeness. It was evident that their connection was fraying, and the memories of their happier times seemed distant and elusive.

As they continued to drift apart, it was a reminder of how complex and fragile relationships could be. The challenge lay in finding a way to bridge the gap, to address the underlying issues that had led to their feuds, and to rebuild the trust and understanding that had once defined their love for each other. Whether they could navigate these challenges and reignite the flame of their relationship remained uncertain.

Mama was already going through a lot, and Grandpa Wade's behavior was over the top. I tried to make her go on walks so that she would be distracted from the hardships she was facing. I made her take Bentley and me to the park, and we played fetch with her. She would throw a frisbee, and we had the very important task of retrieving it for her as fast as we could. However, her laughter was short-lived, and she slipped into her somber mood every time we went back to the house.

I sensed everyone's energy, and it made me feel very down. Bentley and I stopped playing with each other, and it felt as if time stood still in that house. I was an empathetic soul and wanted to make space for people who needed me to be there for them. That's what I did for Mama.

We even played with Papa from time to time to cheer him up. Despite his differences with Mama, he was still our Papa who had rescued us both. We still kind of resented him a little bit for hurting Mama like he did and were taken aback at the fact that he was so nonchalant about the situation. They were drifting apart, and he didn't seem to care.

One day, I was walking in front of their bedroom and heard them speaking in low tones. The door was slightly ajar, so I moved closer to it to hear better. It seemed like they were having a serious discussion.

"We need to do something about our relationship. I just want to know where we went wrong. I wanna know what I did wrong for you to treat me like this."

"Look, you did nothing wrong. It's just... I don't know. This marriage was enforced on me, and I was pretty much coerced into it."

"I didn't know you felt that way," said Mama.

"Well, now you do."

"I think we need to work through this. That is if you want this relationship to work."

"I do. I really do."

"So, I was thinking. We could go to couples counseling. I feel like it would greatly benefit us."

'This is good," I thought to myself. I didn't really know what it was, but it sounded like it would help things get better, and I was all in for it. I rushed to tell Bentley the good news.

He was excited. "I can't wait till things get back to normal," he said to me.

"Me neither."

Mama and Papa went once a week to someone who was called a therapist. They started to talk to each other more. There were actually conversations between them.

It's truly heartbreaking when a relationship reaches a point where hurtful actions persist despite the pain they cause. Despite Mama's wishes, Papa's behavior continued to cause harm to Mama. It's clear that the situation was becoming increasingly unsustainable, and the evidence was mounting that the relationship was bound to fail.

Papa's initial reluctance to engage in the relationship showed that he had reservations from the start. Mama kept trying to bridge the gap, but her efforts were in vain.

When a relationship deteriorates to the point where arguments stop, and communication breaks down, it's a sign that the emotional connection has been tarnished. This is when the gravity of the situation dawns upon everyone.

The journey of investing time, emotions, and energy into a relationship only to face its potential dissolution was incredibly painful for Mama. It forced Mama and Papa to confront the reality that all the hard work, compromise, and shared experiences might be slipping away. The sense of loss and the fear of what the future held was overwhelming.

In such circumstances, seeking clarity about one's own feelings and desires was important. Decisions about whether to continue or end the relationship were made with careful consideration for everyone's well-being. It was a challenging process. Mama had made up her mind. She decided to split from Papa after she had baby Charlotte.

Mama got to transfer back to her old job at Pathpoint, and they were pretty nice to her. They never called her a demon woman or Satan like the other place she worked at. People were always weird with Mama. But she started telling people about the problems she was facing in her marriage. People empathized with her and became sensitive to her plight.

Papa knew this girl from his old band, Sarah, who tricked Mama into being another dog sitter like Jenny. Mama tried to be nice to her, but all the females hated Mama for some reason. I didn't understand it. She could not even kill a fly. She was known for her gentle nature and how kind and generous she was. She was a good person. Well, their loss. They could have found a great friend in Mama, but they were oblivious and she could never understand their behavior.

There was an air of curiosity and anticipation in the household. The familiar scents have shifted, with new and intriguing aromas filling the air. The sounds of excitement and the voices of my family caused a mix of excitement for me. I might not fully understand what was happening, but I could sense the change in the atmosphere.

Mama finally went into labor. She sat up suddenly on the couch as she lay there watching Cupcake Wars on television. She was saying something about her water breaking. Mama started to groan in pain. She doubled over and held her stomach.

"I think I might be in labor! Oh God, it hurts!" she screamed into the phone as she called Grandma.

She was immediately rushed to the hospital. Bentley and I waited, our nervousness building up as we waited for the arrival of our sweet and dear sister to be born.

"I hope she's okay," I said to Bentley.

"She will be. She's strong," he replied.

Grandma came to Mama's aid and helped cut the cord since Papa was at Home Depot then and couldn't make it on time. Bentley and I were so proud of her.

One afternoon, after another round of challenges, Mama made an unexpected decision. Instead of returning home, she expressed her desire to stay at the hospital for a while longer. She wanted to use up all the hospital days on her insurance and did not want to return to Wade and Papa's yelling and threats.

Bentley and I, always by Mama's side, remained vigilant in our plans of guardianship of our little sister once she was home. Our loyalty was unwavering, and we stayed close to Mama, offering both emotional support and a sense of security. Despite the trying circumstances, there was an undeniable beauty in the love and unity that defined our small family.

A lot of Mama and Papa's friends came to visit her. They brought flowers and Mama's favorite chocolates. There was Kent, that demon Sarah SP bassist from hell, and Cammie. Except they didn't let me and Bentley in, so we had to sneak in and look in from the window. She was beautiful a perfect mix of our parents.

"Say hello to our new baby girl Charlotte everyone,"Mama was beeming as a proud mom introduce her daughter for the first time.

"I can't believe it," said Bentley, getting misty-eyed. "Our very own baby sister."

He started to cry with joy as he saw how peaceful she was as she slept. She was absolutely beautiful, and Bentley and I were thrilled. I handed Bentley a paper towel and wiped his eyes.

"Thank you," he said.

Bentley stood by baby Charlotte's side on guard all the time after that. He had a protective nature that was displayed during the times he was needed to fulfill his duties as a loyal companion.

Chapter 6: Mama gets promoted, Enter Satan Nic from Hell. Mama, and Papa Split

Mama moved back into the hell house reluctantly. Papa took time off from Home Depot during his maternity leave. Two months later, Mama was ready to get back to work so she happily returned to PathaPoint and she started working in their day program again like when she first started there. She loved her job and she was excited to be working once again. It's rare to like one's job but I was glad Mama was happy to be there.

Amidst the challenging circumstances, Mama's dedication and hard work brought about a positive transformation in her professional life. She was recognized for her efforts and earned a much-deserved promotion at PathaPoint. This promotion came as she stepped into a role that had previously been held by a stressed individual who ultimately resigned with their first Bed Bug Fiasco at the company's Residential complex.

PathaPoint split his old role into two. She got promoted to Residential Support Plan Coordinator for their Independent Living Program supervising a team of staff while another coworker Christine was promoted to oversee the apartment complex which had six units designated to their clients. Each division was different so Mama's partner was basically Papa's female version which Mama thought was kind of funny.

Papa still hated PathaPoint and I didn't understand what his problem was. He told Mama to work with Sarah as her receptionist. Cammie always pointed out how weird it was that Papa never seemed to understand her jobs.

Papa and Sarah started playing music in the garage religiously alone and she hated it. They were always at it and it disturbed the peace in the house. It also looked inappropriate. To solve the problem, she decided to set her up with their friend Kent. As she hoped, they ended up hitting it off right away. Mama and Papa's frenemies invoked their love for them too which kind of helped her plans.

While Mama was at work, Sarah experienced a miscarriage. Mama recalled her own challenging experience with a miscarriage when she and Papa were trying for a baby. Wanting to offer fertility advice and some empathy, Mama mentioned her past struggle, but Sarah rudely brought up Demon Brent as a weird insult which seemed to set Mama off the deep end. Mama had dealt with similar situations involving certain girls over the years, even noticing a pattern with all of Kent's girlfriends behaving this way. She sighed and rolled her eyes at the predictability.

Mama focused on planning Charlotte's first birthday party, envisioning a Snow White-themed celebration at a charming venue in Northridge Mall. They even had a cute lady dressed as Snow White. The party was a success with everyone joining in the fun, including Grandpa Stuart, who came to visit for the weekend, succeeding in his usual mission to annoy Papa.

One critical moment was when Demon Brent, after all the crazy fights, abruptly removed his drums from the garage without consulting anyone. This sudden action led Papa to mistakenly assume that Mama had a role in the decision, which fueled an intense argument between them. The misunderstanding and accusations escalated the tension within their already strained relationship. There were times when Papa wouldn't come home for days.

I would see them fight a lot and their voices kept getting louder and their attitude toward each other grew more hostile. I was very sensitive to these changes and I found myself moping around in some corner of the house from time to time. Bentley and I would cover our ears with our paws every time we heard Mama and Papa arguing to block out the harsh words they were saying to each other.

As the conflict deepened, Papa's dedication to his band led him to spend extended periods away from home. The emotional distance this created between them intensified Mama's feelings of neglect and isolation. The absence also took a toll on their communication, making it difficult for them to address their issues and find common ground. I understand that Papa's dreams of being a successful musician were valid but it was causing a rift in their relationship. Also, Mama was tired of finding him lieing about his friends not letting him in their Green Day cover band so he could have an excuse to play with Sarah all day basically. That also set Mama off the deep end again when Brent's brother sadly told her the truth. I too, thought it was an embarrassment to their marriage vows. The foundations of their relationship were already unsteady and this attitude of Papa's made it so much worse. I realized that Papa was probably feeling suffocated in the relationship. But what of Mama? What was her fault in all of this?

This series of events gradually eroded the foundation of trust and understanding that Mama and Papa had built over the years. Their relationship became marked by bitterness, unresolved arguments, and a sense of abandonment. The emotional distance between them only seemed to widen as time went on, making it increasingly challenging to mend the fractures in their partnership.

However, over time, due to conflicts with Wade and Papa, Mama's eating habits also started to change. Even Kent and their friends noticed her struggle.

During a double show with their Green Day Cover band and Papa's Standard Profile show, another bassist from hell Satan Nic attempted to pursue Mama using online requests and alluring pictures. He had a strikingly handsome resemblance to Mama's beloved Kurt Cobain with mesmerizing blue eyes.

I questioned Bentley about Nic's intentions, but he just laughed and focused on his mini drum set. Mama's involvement in band practices bothered me. Regrettably, Satan Nic's plan succeeded, leading Mama to deceive Papa about plumbing emergencies at PathPoint, which worried Christine who couldn't help but notice. Mama's department was doing very well at the time while Christine's was suffering with enrollments. However, Christine and other supervisors always stole her staff so Mama could never keep up with all her referrals anyway. Luckily for her, she had a really good team of core staff. Mama also became the Case Magic Nerd Guru which she loved.

Unfortunately one day during a cruise trip to Jamaica with Charlotte, Papa discovered the truth. Papa got a hold of Mama's phone and found the messages between her and Satan Nic. Despite Bentley and I trying to cover for Mama, the situation was unraveling. I felt saddened by the unfolding events and was terrified that Papa might kick Mama out.

Little did I know, she was already several steps ahead of him.

When Mama told Papa she was leaving in their counseling session he didn't believe her.

Satan Nic smartly used this opportunity in the situation. Papa knew his intentions and tried to warn Mama, emphasizing that Satan Nic was even worse than him in their counseling sessions. I believed him, but Mama was angry she didn’t want to hear it. In the past, Papa had manipulated Mama's weight to ensure that no one would be attracted to her, which was also pretty smart.

In a whirlwind of events, Mama kicked Nola, her niece-in-law’s family and Keanu's wife, out of a two-bedroom unit infested with roaches at Grandma’s building. Mama's actions were aggressive, leaving a trail of confusion. The situation escalated quickly. Mama, along with Bentley and baby Charlotte, relocated to that apartment. Papa and I ended up at Troll Grandpa Wade’s. While I was there, I found solace in looking at old family photos, shedding tears for happier times.

Bentley and I exchanged texts, but the connection wasn't the same as before. I longed for the company of my best friends and family. My emotions swung between wanting to blame Mama and Satan Nic, Papa, Grandpa Wade, and even the therapist who seemed to provoke Mama into a frenzied state with her inmate comparisons. I felt as lost as a stray dog again, locked in the garage by Papa alongside rats and spiders. In my frustration, I defiantly marked his band equipment with angry peeing.

Mama's desire for another baby seemed to cloud her judgment as well. Papa's behavior was harsh, and Mama's dreams of a perfect family were shattered, leaving me with the sense that something within her was broken. This left me deeply saddened and heartbroken once more. Occasionally, I spent weekends with Mama, but those moments couldn't fill the void left by the fractured family dynamic

Time started to move quickly Mama and this unexpected love interest added an element of uncertainty to Mama's life, juxtaposing her professional success with personal challenges and new, unexpected connections.

Mama was infatuated with Nic and worked constantly at Pathapoint during these years. Both of them would meet each other like lovers plagued by forbidden love. To Mama, he was the most perfect man in the world. They were both very attracted to one another and Mama had hopes and dreams that he would marry her someday.

I didn't like that Satan Nic at all and I seriously doubted his intentions toward Mama. I had the natural instinct to take care of her. If he broke her heart, I would bite him so hard he would never think of messing with her again.

My visits to Mama, Bentley, and Charlotte were filled with joy and excitement, but as time went on, the ache of separation seemed to intensify rather than diminish. Despite having no constraints on spending time with them, my heart longed for more. I was a dog driven by pure affection, and my love for my family was unwavering, but the circumstances kept us apart.

In the midst of their physical absence, I found myself grappling with an unspoken yearning to bridge the gap between us and to be part of their lives. My canine heart was laden with complex emotions.

The days seemed to pass with a sense of melancholy that hung over me like a cloud. The toys and spaces once shared with Bentley and Charlotte now stood as silent reminders of what once was. Every wag of my tail was tinged with a touch of sadness and I'm sure my eyes mirrored my emotions. I barely played because what was even the point of playing alone? Why would it be fun if I couldn't share my toys with anyone? If I had no one to snuggle with? Honestly, Papa's behavior with Mama and his indifference pulled me away from him. So I withdrew into my shell. Papa tried his best to take me out for walks but they weren't as enjoyable as they were before. I remembered how Bentley would play as

Charlotte watched from her stroller. I missed all the good times we had together but now I felt desolate.

But amidst the sorrow, there was also determination. My loyalty knew no bounds, and the bond I shared with my family was a driving force. In my own simple way, I began to seek solace in the familiar scents they left behind, finding comfort in the traces of Mama, Bentley, and Charlotte that lingered in the air.

I would curl up in Mama's favorite chair, finding solace in the residual warmth she had left. The sound of my paws against the floor became a dance of remembrance, echoing the playful romps I once shared with my family. And as the days turned into weeks, my presence seemed to weave itself into the very fabric of the household, a constant reminder that love endures even in absence.

Papa wasn't actively trying to reconcile with Mama, but they still did a few things together with Charlotte as a family. It was good that she received love and affection from both her parents.

Since he was not living with Mama, Satan Nic would sneak in at night. Mama once suspected he had a girlfriend and would obsessively stalk her online. This person resembled Sarah, named Abigal with pale skin and dark hair, which made Mama sad and angry. Then to Mama's surprise, she found out that the mean girls Auntie Norma, Daniella, and Laura, were all discussing her behind her back online. It was all madness. I'm glad I couldn't be involved in these dramas. There are perks of being a dog, I have to admit.

Mama meanwhile was "killing it" as humans say at PathaPoint enjoying her fun grant-funded projects and even joining a leadership program. However, she was not truly happy because she wanted a family with either Nic or Papa. She just wanted another baby. She even looked into adopting until her family and friends started calling her "Mommy Dearest."

Bentley and I during this time became Charlotte's loyal doggy companions, forming an inseparable bond with her. Our dedication to keeping her company and ensuring she was always cared for showcased our unwavering commitment to her well-being. We went above and beyond to lessen any feelings of solitude and vulnerability she might have experienced.

The interactions between Charlotte and her doggy brothers were heartwarming and endearing. As she made her first attempts at movement, Bentley and I looked over her with a watchful eye, ready to play and offer encouragement. The sight of her attempting to crawl and the sound of her giggles brought immeasurable joy to us. Her innocent laughter resonated as a source of pure happiness, serving as a reminder of the simple pleasures in life.

Every little gesture and action of Charlotte amplified the depth of our connection. Her gurgles and playful sounds became a language of our own, nurturing an even stronger sense of understanding between us. We responded with enthusiasm, making sure she felt loved and supported at every step of her journey. Bentley loved to hang by her high chair as she threw food down for him. He slept in her toy teepee tent as she played with her Barbies and Trolls. He followed her around like a loyal guardian.

In return, Charlotte's affection toward us was evident in her radiant smile and the sparkle in her eyes whenever we were around. The unconditional love she felt for us mirrored our devotion to her. Through our interactions, a unique and heartwarming bond was formed, creating cherished memories that would last a lifetime.

As time went on, her growth and development continued to be a source of wonder for us. Her progress, no matter how small, was proof of the nurturing environment we had collectively created. Our roles as guardians and friends were beautifully intertwined. This demonstrated the profound impact that animals can have on human lives, especially in fostering feelings of companionship, protection, and happiness.

Chapter 7: Bentley dies of Covid, Illinois Crisis with Grandpa. Papa gets pissed at Mama (again)

One day, as I was lounging around in Mama's old chair, Papa walked in with a somber expression on his face. It looked as if he had seen a ghost. I was immediately concerned and wondered what was going on. I perked up my ears and trotted toward him, whining. I wanted to know what had happened that had Papa so distressed. I licked his hand and looked up into his eyes with concern, somehow trying to find an answer. Still, I got no response from him as he plopped down on the couch in the living room.

Then to my sheer alarm, I saw tears forming in his eyes. I whined again, cuddling up to him. I wanted to comfort him even though I had no idea what had happened.

"Good boy, Wallace," he said as he stroked my fur. I wanted to ask him, but I didn't know how to get my message across.

"It's Bentley," he said but trailed off.

'What about Bentley?' I wondered to myself.

"Your friend, boy. He's gone."

'What does he mean gone? Was he given away?' I thought to myself.

"COVID got him, Wallace."

'Got him? What is he talking about?'

I kept staring at Papa till he spoke more. I nudged his arm with my nose in an attempt to let him know that I was listening. I cocked my head to get a further response from him.

"He's dead, Wallace! he said out loud and placed his head in his hands, and broke down. His shoulders shook as he cried.

'Dead? How can he be dead?' I thought to myself. 'No, this can't be true. There has to be some sort of misunderstanding.'

Papa's words resonated in my mind, and I tried to make sense of what he was telling me. 'Nah, there's no way.'

However, as I watched him cry, dread started to boil in my gut. 'It's true. Why else would he cry like this if it wasn't true?'

I realized that I was in denial. My best friend, my companion, could not have left me. Not when I needed him the most. 'How could he?' I thought angrily. I started to whine even louder at the news, and tears began to fall from my eyes.

Papa kept stroking my head, trying to calm me down. 'It's okay, boy. You're going to be okay," he said.

'No, I'm not,' I thought.

I wanted to see Bentley so badly, and I had been waiting for the time when we would finally meet and play together. I couldn't bear not to have him there. I didn't want to feel his absence. I couldn't take it.

'I hope I can see him one last time,' I thought.

Papa called Mama and asked if he could bring me to her house to say my final goodbye to Bentley. "I think he understood. He has such a strong intuition," he said with tears still in his eyes. I couldn't hear what Mama was saying on the other end, but I gathered that I was going to go and see my best friend for the last time. I whined and scratched at Papa's leg.

"Let's go, buddy," he said, running to fetch my leash.

I had a knot in my stomach as I had never seen anyone dead before. I was a little scared, too, but I knew it was necessary for me to see him one last time.

As we reached Mama's house, she looked disheveled. It looked like she had been crying for hours, but the look of how swollen her eyes were. She reached down and picked me up, burying her face in my neck, and started to sob. "Oh, my baby," she choked out. "I'm so glad you are here," she said, her voice muffled against my coat. " I am so sorry."

When Mama took me inside the house, she took me to Bentley's bed, and sure enough, he was there, lying limp. His eyes were closed. The room started to spin. I thought I was ready, but I truly wasn't. I started to howl and ran over to Bentley's body, walking in circles around him to depict my sorrow and the pain of my loss.

Seeing me like this made everyone cry. Charlotte, who was now grown enough to understand what death was, started to bawl. Mama and Papa rushed to comfort her, leaving me to stare down at Bentley.

The world was so cruel. How could my best friend be taken from me? The only one I loved and trusted. 'My poor brother,' I thought to myself. 'He didn't deserve this.'

It was almost as if Bentley was going to wake up and say that he was playing a prank on us. It felt as if he was going to get up and start spreading chaos like he always used to do. The trait of him which annoyed me was now needed. I longed for my friend to get up and start playing with me, but he was dead. Never to move or be around me again. Never to be able to play with Charlotte and me.

I ran to Charlotte in an attempt to provide her with the love she got from Bentley. I thought maybe I could fill the void in her little heart.

Mama and Papa got Bentley cremated. As they got the ashes, they cried till they couldn't anymore.

In the solitude of Papa's house, a heavy blanket of sorrow lay thick over me. I sat on the ledge of the window, looking outside at the lawn. In my mind's eye, I could see me and Bentley running and playing there. My heart yearned to play with him just once more, but the thought of never being able to see him again was like a knife in my heart.

Charlotte was desolate. She stopped playing and eating, sparking concern from her mother. She tried her best to cheer her up, but her heart was aching too. She would give her many kisses and cuddles whenever she could.

Bentley, everyone's companion, had been a source of boundless joy for everyone, but Mama's vibrant house felt empty, as if there was a large vacuum in the house. The echoes of the pitter-patter of his paws were still settled into the walls.

I knew it would take a long time to be able to get used to him not being around, but at the time, it was agonizing.

I was moved back with Mama and Charlotte, and this was a source of comfort for me. At least I had my little sister to share my pain with. At least I had Mama to cuddle me and comfort me during this difficult time.

Life goes on, and Mama, after finishing her grant-funded furniture from her time at the non-profit organization.

The worst thing she feared to happen happened. Papa had found a new love interest. She was a red-haired thing who was a lot prettier than Mama. She had flashbacks of when Papas friend Valerie told her his new girlfriend was cooler and didn't look like she had Down's Syndrome. Satan Nic also began verbally abusing Mama saying she was trans, retarted, and that he didn't love her. Mama was shocked when Cammie told her she was just a child's plaything. It seemed like Mama was not a fit for this group anymore. It caused so much confusion and stress. Mama would cry her eyes out all the time, invoking concern from me and Charlotte.

Once, Mama took Charlotte to Papa's house and created a scene by throwing a brick on the floor and ripping a snoopy sticker off the window. Charlotte later came home crying, and Papa got pissed at Mama.

"You have to go to the mental hospital again," he told her with anger in his eyes. "You are not stable." He also threatened Mama in the past not to ask for more money or he'd tell the judge she was crazy having her sign papers with shady lawyers.

These people always wanted her there and to live there. When Mama was taken there, the doctor told us that she was okay and that she could go back to work. They told her no one should have taken her daughter from her. However, everything was fine for a while before she got depressed again after a few months. I could tell that she was bored at Pathapoints too.

I saw her graduate from the leadership program. There were times she would be taking Zoom calls, and I would sit by her side, trying to make sense of what was happening. I even helped her with invoices during the time of the pandemic. Another man left at PathaPoint, and her boss Marla offered her another promotion and opportunity but Mama didn't think that was the right Path for her as money and another title really wasn't giving her much happiness. Although she was very appreciative of them.

During this time, when Mama was so busy, Grandpa Stuart would pick fights with her over and over from Chicago. One day she was about to give a presentation for Autism Awareness Month when Grandpa Stuart from Chicago sent her numerous photos of the Serial Killer Monster calling her a lesbian once more and Mila Kunis on meth saying "Awareness Day." Mama quit instantly afraid and confused. She's never been a drug addict, never even was a party girl. Her other boss Glenda along with Marla reached out to see if she was okay and convinced her to go back. She could not get any peace. She got threatened by Papa's old friends constantly threatening to put her in jail or at the mental hospital. For years she called 211 to report their abuse as well as threatening to take Charlotte away. Papa was clearly making Mama look like a bad person in front of them too. Mama was also concerned Papa spent Thanksgiving with these people after they threatened her about Charlotte.

As time went on, a few months later after being attacked from more of their old friends Mama decided to got a job at Illinois Crisis Prevention Network, similar to PathaPoint. Right before she left they could tell she was burnt out as they had a zoom meeting with nice supervisors in other divisions who could sense Mama was going to move on. Since covid, she got lots of job offers but decided on Illinois Crisis Prevention. She wanted to get away from the violence and threats. Cammie and Laura had sent Uncle Ronnie to attack her along with his friend making her feel very unsafe and traumatized. Another friend from Mama's past Sonya and Launy who moved into Auntie Nora's would tell Mama disturbing comments her sister made about her. Sonya also was verbally abusive to Mama and when the Emma Stone Cruella came out they all started bullying her again. They always liked to call her ugly. Mama was always compared to Cruella through the years which she kind of liked. San Bernadino Police once said lock her up and throw away the key. Mama took Charlotte to see the new Cruella and loved it. That seemed to bother them even more. Sonya even had an episode in Mama's apartment once I was there. They also loved to call Mama a psycho.

So fast forward again Mama liked Illinois Crisis, but she was still depressed and shocked by the strange attacks. Also, Grandpa Stuart wouldn't let up and kept fighting with her when he should have been watching Charlotte. Uncle Ronnie was still fighting her from CA threatening her on the phone. Mama was initially only going to PathaPoints part-time, but with time they kept giving her work till she practically began to live there but she loved the chaos and joy it brought to her life. So, going back to a normal 9-5 in an office was hard for her.

Grandpa still didn't understand and never kept his mouth shut. He was such a lazy man that he slept all day as I stayed with him till Mama got back from work. He was supposed to be watching Charlotte while Mama was at work but he was having a sad temper tantrum leaving Charlotte to play on her tablet. He would complain about me peeing on everything. But I wanted to have my revenge like Mama on him in my way. This is a doggy way of saying, "Do not mess with me."

'Come on, Grandpa. I'm Wallace! I don't care!' I thought.

Once, when Mama took me for a walk, I saw someone who looked like Papa playing basketball with another guy and began to cry and whine because I missed him. I still stayed positive and played with Charlotte in the snow, having the time of my life. I knew I had to stay strong for her and never give up on my duty to keep her happy and entertained.

"Come on, Wallace! I'm going to take you someplace special," said Grandpa out of the blue one day. Following that, he took me and Charlotte to the Easter Fest, where we had a lot of fun. I got to hang out with the Easter Bunny and get extra treats. I started to bond with Grandpa as he would take me on walks with him to pick up Charlotte from school.

Mama started working for Uber Eats around the clock soon after, allowing me to spend time with Grandpa and Charlotte at the park. Our condo was great, Mama got Grandpa a fancy leather couch from Ashley Furniture and a new bedroom set for Charlotte too.. We also bought some witchcraft items to start a new blessing in the condo. Unfortunately, it didn't seem to work well, as my Mama faced harassment from the police and social workers while doing Uber deliveries like she was a criminal. This made her job extremely difficult. Charlotte who loved My Little Pony laughed at one of the police officers Hitch who was chasing around a magical creature, which reminded her of the situation. Those social workers and police officers meant well I'm sure.

"I don't wanna go to school!" Charlotte cried one day. She didn't like going to school, and all she wanted to do was stay at home and play that stupid Roblox game. She was angry that Mama took her away from her favorite Grandma and her cousins. However, Mama would see Charlotte and Grandpa laugh together. They enjoyed watching TV and eating together. That made Mama smile. Somehow Charlotte made it through school successfully and Grandpa at least seemed to enjoy his time with her.

One day out of the blue the social worker ladies came to our house. One of these characters was afraid of me, so they locked me in the bathroom. They would disrespect Mama, who got extremely pissed, and she told them to screw themselves respectfully, and then she told Grandpa that she was busy with work, so he should shut up and take care of Charlotte. She was used to Grandma helping her all the time while she went back and forth at PathaPoint for years and didn't understand how lazy Grandpa was.

They didn't stop, though. They harassed Mama once again and told her to come back to the condo. I felt a rage within me because of how my Mama was accused of things she didn't even do seeing she used her 403b money from PathaPoint for the Condo and had kitchen remodeling plans. One day, channeling

Bentley's energy, I jumped off the couch and attacked a social worker woman. After all, I had to protect my loved ones from this nonsense.

Finding out about this, Papa flew in from California because he was mad at Mama and took Charlotte back with him. This was devastating for Mama again.

When Mama asked evil Grandma if she could stay with her, she refused heartlessly. There was a little ghetto boy in the building who had a crush on Mama so she didn't want to stay there anyway and be bothered by Auntie Nora's harassment after she moved into the building. They liked to pretend Mama was a lesbian for some reason and have men harass her like Uncle Ronnie. He was now on a rampage because he was womanless taking his anger out on Mama too. He even said he'd beat her up on the streets when she was back in the valley. He had completely lost it. Mama terrified tried to stay at Demon Brent's garage but was threatened by Laura who originally was part of that initial attack using Ronnie and his minion friend. She called her friends at 211 and they let her know about a safe parking lot in Reseda she could stay at. She kept trying to get Papa to let her stay with him, but he said no as well. She really didn't want to fight with them either at the hell house.

Doing Uber Eats in California kept her busy during the tragedy. Thanks to something called Prop 22, she was getting extra money every two weeks that they didn't have in Illinois, so that was a plus. She still missed Pathapoint, though, and would often check in with her friend Amanda, who still worked there. Uber was a big blessing to our family and our silver lining in this situation. She still sent Grandpa Stuart money for the Condo, fighting Papa to make him give Evil Grandma money while he was controlling Charlotte's and the family's time together.

As days went by, Mama decided to propose to Papa once more, so she began to plan a big Cruella Christmas thinking maybe this was a sign for her family to get back together. We had a wonderful summer Mama planned the best activities for her, Papa and Charlotte. My favorite was the special doggy night at Warner Center watching Paw Patrol. She even threw the cutest My Little Pony party for Charlotte at the park and had the Hocus Pocus witches surprise everyone for Halloween. So her big plan was to have a Cruella Christmas Eve where she proposed to Papa with her family around. She bought everyone extra presents even for the frenemies. Mama also went all out and dressed as the Emma Stone Cruella and hired the original as well with Mickey and Minnie to help her pass out the gifts to everyone. Somehow, deep inside, she knew that Papa would say no. One day while Mama was working out at the gym, Papa yelled at her "I don't love you!"

Mama always ten steps ahead of Papa got her and Grandma Cruella and Evil Queen rings, gifting Papa a Cruella watch instead. She even got fancy purses for her sister Kate Spade even for gossipy sis-in-law Evelyn. She also found a Bentley limo and a Bentley dog, but Grandpa Wade was a major party pooper, canceled it at his house, and tried to kick out Papa although this could be another lie to Mama as he just partied at the house with Uncle Ronnie's ex-girlfriend and their friends for Thanksgiving. Luckily Auntie Norma let us have the party at her house which now was at Grandma's building.

For this, Papa blamed Mama once more. It seemed as if they would never cease to fight, and honestly, it was becoming tiring to witness. I didn't even have anyone to discuss this with now that Bentley was dead. The replacement could never be him, and I never warmed up to him.

Aunt Norma watched little Bentley with adoration in her eyes and asked Mama if she could keep him for her kids.

"Yeah, cool," said Mama. "He can be everyone's dog."

Grandpa Wade, being as evil as he is, didn't let me go to the backup party hosted by Mama and locked me in the garage alone like I was Cinderella's dog or something. I was extremely upset and kept crying, looking at old photographs. It seemed as if the sorrow would never end at that moment.

However, the next day, I got to see Mama, Papa, and Charlotte and was happy again. It seemed like we, as dogs, always learn to adapt to any situation since we are very smart animals. It doesn't take a lot for us to be happy. All we need is our families by our side, and we will be the most joyous creatures on earth. We cherish all of these moments with all of our hearts. What more could a dog ask for?

Mama surprised me with extra treats and Cruella dog toys as I watched Charlotte open her presents. I imagined Bentley and Lexi would be looking down upon us from heaven and smiling. I could almost feel their presence around us.

Chapter 8: I pass away to Heaven, meet Lexi

In the face of uncertainty, Mama's resilience and ability to adapt were commendable. Her commitment to creating a safe and nurturing environment for her family, even in the face of challenges, demonstrated her love and dedication to her loved ones.

If there was anything Mama hated, it was people trying to poke their noses into her business and her life choices. She scanned the neighborhood painstakingly to make sure no one was trying to approach her with warmth but had the willingness to snoop around in her life and interfere with her process. She was not going to sit around and let people in because she had had enough of them and their attitude toward her. She wanted to make sure that it was safe and didn't have her crazy friends attack her again. Mama was paying for furniture at Grandpa's condo in IL and Grandpa Wade's abandoned and ugly house. Mama thought a furnished co-living place made the most sense at this time.

Charlotte wanted to spend time with her cousins at grandma's house. However, in the midst of all of her struggles, Mama reached a breaking point. She was tired of constantly moving and buying furniture due to all the threats and violence over the years. To put an end to the instability, she considered the co-living situation. This decision stemmed from her frustration with excessive drama and demands from friends and family who never supported her. Mama went back to CA and sent them all Applebee gift cards, encouraging them to hang out together. But they all engaged in bizarre disappearing acts, adding to her stress and prompting her to prioritize her own well-being as well as Charlotte's.

She was on the verge of renting an apartment in Chatsworth, which even had a dog park for little old me, when something terrible happened.

One day, I woke up and saw Papa standing over me and crying. I got up and took a few steps, trying to figure out what had gone wrong. As soon as I turned I saw my body lying motionless near his feet.

'What the heck is going on?' I wondered. 'Why can I see myself sleeping?'

Initially, I thought I was just having sleep paralysis and waited for myself to wake up. A long time went by as I stood beside Papa and watched him cry.

'Why am I not waking up? What is going on?'

Papa was looking at my body and I wanted to jump into his arms and lick his face. The sight of my body was both surreal and haunting, my existence reduced to a fragile vessel devoid of the spark that once set it alive.

I grappled with different emotions. I pondered the mysteries of existence and the etherial boundaries that defined it. I realized that my journey was far from over as the veil between the two realities thinned, and a whisper of hope echoed, suggesting that my story maybe had more chapters to reveal. I decided that I was not going to leave my family no matter what.

Papa's voice quivered with emotions. His usual steady tone was now a reflection of the pain within. As tears blurred his vision, he reached for his phone, his fingers trembling as he dialled Mama's number. The weight of the news he was about to share was unbearable, evident in the way he struggled to steady his breath before speaking.

With each word, his voice cracked. The ache in his heart was evident in every word.

"Ashley..." he began.

For some reason, I could hear Mama's voice crystal clear through his phone.

"Hey, everything okay?" she asked. "Are you crying?!"

"It's Wallace," he began, his voice cracking once again. "He's dead."

"What? How?!" Mama exclaimed. "Are you sure he's dead?"

"I woke up and just saw him like this. I don't know what happened!" cried Papa. He was hiccupping now, unable to form sentences.

The air around me felt like it was thickening. The gravity of his words, hanging heavy as if the atmosphere absorbed his sorrow. I could also hear Mama crying on the other end. My life had been cut short. I had so many things to do. I had to be there for my family. For Mama. For Charlotte. I couldn't imagine not being in their arms for the rest of their lives, as long as they lived. The thought that I wouldn't be able to see them as I crossed over to the afterlife was heart-wrenching.

The world around me seemed to blur as the reality of the situation sank in. My death was a mysterious enigma and became the center of whispers and hushed conversations. I couldn't understand any of it. I found myself in a realm between reality and the unknown. As if in a daze, I wandered through the veil that separated life from the afterlife.

All of a sudden, I heard a beautiful sound and saw Lexi floating down to me on a cloud.

"Lexi, what is this?!" I asked her.

"Wallace, you passed away last night and I have come to take you to heaven with me." She replied, with a grave expression on her face.

"What? No! I can't go! Mama, Papa, and Charlotte need me now more than ever! Mama was going to take me to the dog park!"

"Sorry, Wallace I was sad too to leave everyone but you still will be able to look out for them in heaven."

"Heaven?"

"Yes and we get to be together in heaven like you always wanted."

"Okay, Lexi take me to see Mama, Charlotte and Papa together one last time."

Lexi and I floated to the park where Mama and Papa told Charlotte I passed away. They got her some treats and they all hugged and cried. I had tears in my eyes because I wanted to console my sister. I watched them all for a long time before I felt Lexi nudge me with her nose. "Let them mourn," she spoke. "It's important for them to feel these feelings and learn how to deal with them. Grief is a funny thing. It takes you through so many emotional roller coasters. Right now the gravity of the situation probably hasn't settled in but don't worry. I believe they will be fine. Life goes on. It's okay, Wallace, see how good of a dog you were they loved you so much."

"Thanks, Lexi. I miss them already."

"I know I missed them so much too when I crossed over, but there is nothing you can do about it. Of course, I still looked over you guys and prayed for you every day."

"That is so sweet of you," said Wallace.

"It is truly my duty to watch over my humans."

"What about Bentley, why isn't he here?"

"Well Wallace, that's what I have to tell you next. Bentley did not make it to heaven because he chose to go to hell."

"What?! Why?!"

"Well he wanted to pursue other things at this time and he became very close to Satan," said Lexi. "He liked the nickname Demon Dog and he's been hanging down there a lot joking and having fun."

"Oh my God, that sounds like Bentley living his dream life," I sighed. "Can we at least see him?"

"Sure I'll take you," said Lexi.

Meanwhile Mama Amidst this process, found a confidante in her case manager who called her Ashely creepily like her old boss at PathaPoint. Despite the aggressive quirks, Mama developed a trusting relationship with 211 Safe Parking and confided in them about her situation and plans.

They assisted Mama in securing the downpayment for this co-living apartment Mama found like her old office. Since I had passed away Mama was depressed and didn't see the point in getting an apartment with a dog park or dog wash. This apartment, located at 211 Safe Parking, became the focal point of Mama's alternate plan. It was clear that Mama's determination to secure a stable living arrangement for her family was unwavering. Charlotte did not want to stay at Papa's and was to problem-solve again she figured Charlotte was happy at Grandma's with her cousins. Mama can't stand the violence towards her. She would continue to meet Papa and Charlotte two days a week and figured she could get a more expensive place when Charlotte's older and out of debt from all this furniture. The police told her to just make a paper trail of the violence but no real solution to the problem. Papa also doesn't have the ability to keep anyone safe. I felt bad I wasn't there with her and how everyone was treating her. I was happy to have Lexi meet me with Bentley to see if he had any ideas to help.

Chapter 9: Bentley and Wallace Meet Again

I had found myself in a different realm. It was almost as if I was waiting for this moment his entire life. For instance, I was just a lone traveler going through the paces of life only to arrive at this moment in the end. This was unlike anything he had experienced, The air was filled with otherworldly luminescence, casting a soft and ethereal glow upon the vast landscape. The ground beneath my paws felt solid yet it seemed as if I was levitating over it.

As I looked around, I realized that this was a place where the boundaries between the real world and the afterlife blurred. This was the place where your fate was decided.

"This is beautiful," said Wallace to Lexi.

"I know right? I find drifting here and there quite fun," she replied. "Of course, heaven is entirely something else. You'll know in a minute when you see it. I don't understand why Bentley even likes hell. Maybe it's because he loves chaos. Always has. I didn't think he would change in the afterlife either."

We passed by massive golden gates that I assumed were leading to heaven. As I wandered from near it toward hell, I noticed a vibrant landscape that stretched out in every direction, from rolling hills covered in iridescent flowers and the horizon covered in crystal clear lakes that seemed to mirror the skies above and below simultaneously. The colors there were more vivid than anything I had seen on Earth. It was as if every hue was brighter and more intense. It felt as if I had been floating in a dream before I died, but now this felt more real and palpable as compared to Earth. I realized I was just standing there, watching the mesmerizing scene. He never wanted anything more than to just spend the rest of eternity there.

"Wallace?" I heard Lexi's voice. "We gotta move forward. We came come back later."

As we wandered further, I saw silver gates, behind which I could see flickering fire and smelled smoke.

Bentley had also transitioned to this plane but his heart was drawn to a unique path.

"He has formed a relationship with Satan and he wants to acquire his perspectives and profound wisdom," explained Lexi. "I have got to say that Satan has changed a lot. He has the perfect balance of light and darkness and wants the kingdom of hell to benefit from his knowledge."

Satan, in this realm, had transformed into a figure of neutrality, no longer embodying the traditional concepts of good and evil. Instead, he was an individual who fostered growth and change. He was no longer a fearsome figure but a friend. The friendship of Bentley and Satan was an embodiment of the unexpected connections that could be formed in this new world.

I could hear rock music blaring along the flames as we walked by. I couldn't make out the lyrics but I knew for sure that it was some satanic mumbo jumbo about taking the throne from the tyrant that they refer to as God. I had heard quite a bit of rock and metal music thanks to Bentley and Papa. I used to hate it in the beginning but it grew on me with time. However, I didn't agree with the lyrics most of the time.

"Lexi, this is very nice I bet Bentley loves this," I spoke.

We made our way to a fancy gate with gargoyles. Lexi barked and a little demon with a goat head entered.

"We are here to see Bentley the dog," she announced.

"Hold on," said the demon. "I will call him. What unit number?"

"Demon dog 666," replied Lexi.

The guard checked on the tablet. "Just give me a moment," he said and waddled inside. He picked up his cell phone and dialed a number on it. "Sir, you have two dogs here Lexi and Wallace that have come to visit you." I figured it was Bentley. He told him to let us in.

"Okay you may enter," said the demon.

"Check this out," said Lexi and nodded her head toward a hot pink car that was parked outside the gates.

"This is such a funny car," I said and laughed. "What are you, Barbie?"

"Thanks," Lexi rolled her eyes.

We took Lexi's little pink car down and we drove inside. Then out of nowhere, a low growl rumbled through the air. Suddenly a dog with three heads appeared in front of the car.

The dog was unlike anything had seen before. Its three heads towered above the car. Each head possessed a different personality. The middle head appeared to be the leader. It spoke in a deep and echoing voice. "Where do you think you're going?"

"Cerebrus, we just want to pass through," said Lexi.

"I want an offering," the middle head spoke while the other two growled at us."

"We don't have anything. You know it's kind of hard to have material things in this realm. I'm sorry but we can't help you," said Lexi calmly.

I was surprised at how composed she was and how firm she was with such a monstrous creature. Her calm demeanor struck me. Her unwavering courage in the face of this mythical creature shocked me.

I realized I was shaking. 'I wonder what will happen if he attacks us? It's not like we can die once more,' I thought to myself.

"Don't worry, Wallace. He won't do anything," said Lexi to me. Then she turned to Cerebrus. "Would you like some pets instead?" She offered.

The dog walked up to the car and Lexi extended her paw out to scratch each of its head one by one. Cerebrus closed his eyes and had a goofy smile on his face. The fearsome guardian looked harmless in this situation. The growls dissolved into contented sighs, and an almost childlike joy took over Cerebrus.

'Phew,' I thought to myself.

In that surreal moment, I realized the power of empathy and connection. Lexi's simple act of kindness and affection had transformed the formidable obstacle into a moment of unexpected peace.

With a sense of accomplishment, Lexi withdrew her paw and Cerebrus reluctantly stepped back from the car. After the ordeal was over, Lexi drove on. I couldn't help but admire Lexi's ability to bridge the gap between the ordinary and the extraordinary, demonstrating that even in the most difficult of circumstances, compassion and understanding could prevail.

This was a realm of suffering known as "Inferna." The air was thick with the scent of burning sulphur and the sky was a perpetual maelstrom of fire. Rivers of molten metal flowed through jagged landscapes, casting an eerie glow upon the boulders that stretched as far as the eye could see. People contorted and writhed in agony as their flesh burned off their bones like candle wax.

Malevolent creatures with twisted forms and gnarled limbs roamed the land, feeding off the misery of the damned. Towering citadels made of obsidian and bone loomed in the distance, their spires reaching toward the heavens only to be taken over by the flames.

As the car floated to its destination, I heard the screaming sounds emanating from the flames all around us. "What's going on?" I asked Lexi.

"These are the tormented souls. These people committed grave crimes that are unforgivable. Now they are doomed to serve an entire eternity in the hellfire."

"That's terrifying!" I exclaimed.

"Adolf Hitler is one of the most famous ones in this realm. The holocaust was one of the most harrowing acts in history. He will never be forgiven. Each day here is a cycle of painful torment. A nightmare without end. Where the existence of one's being is eroded by the unrelenting fury of this land."

"Well," I said. "I'm glad I'm not that guy.

"You could not. You are one of the sweetest dogs I know. There is no way you could end up in hell," replied Lexi. "Besides dogs are always pure and free of sin. All we do is be there for our owners and our friends and that is reward enough for us. What else do we do anyway?"

"You're so right. I made sure I was a good boy throughout my life."

Despair in hell enveloped every soul. The concept of escape is a far cry. The boundaries of Inferna seemed to be endless, and the suffering never stopped.

We drove in silence for a few moments.

"Hey, Lexi," I said, breaking the heavy silence.

"Yes?"

"I'm worried for Mama, Papa, and Charlotte."

"I know the feeling but there is nothing we can do. All we can do is say a prayer for them so that they may remain safe and happy."

Tears started to form in my eyes as I imagined what it would have been like for them to find my lifeless body. Their good boy was gone forever but I didn't want to be the reason for their grief. Still, this was what life is about. Things change and people leave. The cycle just continues even after one is gone.

A bittersweet ache formed in my heart. Their companion who had stuck with them through thick and thin was now gone. The cycle of change and loss marched forward relentlessly. Even after one's physical presence faded away.

Emotions swirled within me. The sadness for the pain of the absence they may face. I wished there was a profound longing to comfort them, someone, to let them know that my love and loyalty would forever remain with them. Life was cruel and this was a bitter pill to swallow, it was a reminder that everything is temporary. Yet, amidst this somber truth, there was a slight glimmer of solace. The power of love and the memories would forever bind us together.

We slowed down and she made a turn down Demon Street and stopped in front of a crazy little house with Satanic metal music blasting. The house was black with blood-red shingles adorned over every window. The architecture of the house was poor and it looked like it was designed by an imbecile. The construction was crooked and all wrong.

We walked out and Lexi rang the doorbell. "BENTLEY" She called.

There was a commotion inside before Bentley opened the door. I was so glad to see him. A rush of emotions overtook me and I realized I was crying as I ran to give him a long hug.

“Oh my God, my friends! Come in, come in!” Bentley wiped a tear from his eye with his paw.

He was wearing a robe with little flames and skulls. On the walls were a bunch of ridiculous self-portraits of him, and some cute ones of him and Mama, him and Charlotte. There were some weird artistic photos of him biting Papa from different angles I can't help but laugh. I stopped at the one of me and him. “Bentley I love this art photo,” I spoke.

“Thank you Wallace I got that especially made. I'm happy in my new little home in hell. I get along with Satan pretty well.”

“I'm not surprised Bentley my friend. We all sat around and Bentley ordered food for us. “What would you guys like...”

Lexi interrupted. “Bentley, now that Wallace is back. We'd like to talk to you. We want you to join us in heaven.”

"Yes, Bentley I want to get our family back together again. We want you to get your dog wings," I added.

"Ummm. I don't think it's going to work Wallace. It's been 7 years. Too much Broomfield nonsense," responded Bentley.

"I know Bentley but Papa Mama and Charlotte need us to help them. Don't you want to earn your wings and join us?"

"No, I like it here and Satan has our satanic Sunday sangrias, and I help him with little projects. We play cards on Tuesdays etc I don't want to leave him he's been a good friend."

"What better than me, Bentley?" I asked. I was hurt and jealous that my best friend had a new friend.

"Ummm, okay, Wallace. As long as I can still visit Satan and hang with him sometimes, I'll come with you guys." Replied Bentley, uncertainty lacing his words.

"Yes! Perfect, Wallace, let's do this!" I exclaimed a mixture of excitement and relief evident in my voice.

Bentley, his little face scrunched up in thought, turned to me with big eyes and asked, "Will you promise to play with me and Lexi every day?"

I looked at Bentley and gave him a warm smile. "For as long as you want," I assured him.

Lexi chimed in, her voice gentle and comforting. "Just come with us. We'll have fun days every day and nothing will ever change. We will be happy for all eternity. Plus you can always come back here whenever you feel fit."

Bentley's expression changed to that of curiosity. He tilted his head, thinking deeply. "Hmmm, I'm listening. Sounds interesting."

"Bentley, imagine all the adventures we could have. We'll explore new places, play games, and laugh together every day. You know what? We can even invite Satan to join us sometimes, so you won't have to miss out on your friendship with him."

"And think of all the treats we will be getting! Think of all the friends we can make! You'll have an endless number of playmates, and every day will be a new and exciting experience!"

"Well, I do like me some treats and friends," said Bentley with wonder and awe on his face. He seemed enchanted with the idea of heaven.

"Exactly. So come with us."

"Well, you have me convinced. Let's do this!"

Chapter 10: Proposal Plan gone wrong. BENTLEY SNEAKS ALTERNATE ENDING.

Before we knew it, it was Springtime in the valley. Once again, the flowers were blooming while my family was still mourning my passing. Mama was getting adjusted to her new non-dog friendly co-living place while Charlotte was enjoying her time with Grandma and her cousins.

This time, Papa got into a big car accident, and Mama was taking him to work and Charlotte to school. She was grateful to work Uber Eat deliveries while she was her family's transportation system. Mama was so happy she wanted to plan another fun holiday surprise for her family. She and her friends loved playing Super Mario together through the years. She was excited to get Charlotte into playing the classics, Mario Kart especially. She and Papa were not too comfortable with a lot of the Roblox games and some of the kids she was playing with online.

"Roy, Charlotte was fighting some kid the other day, they bully each other. It's not good," Mama played 'Adopt Me' with Charlotte and would witness some disturbing things. Although it seemed more cute than bad, but it wasn't as wholesome as the classics.

"Universal Studios is opening up a Mario world, and the new movie is coming out. For Easter this year,

I'm going to get her a Nintendo Switch from the Easter Bunny; you buy the Mario Stuffed animals from Build a Bear." Charlotte wanted a real bunny, but a stuffed one was the next best thing.

Mama was also happy with the new movie as she loved the cast. "Well, take her to see the new movie that'll be our priming." This was a Glenda word; her old boss used it at times in their monthly meetings when they'd discuss difficult clients' behaviors and brainstorm. It was often a way to slowly introduce a desired behavior.

"Okay," Papa agreed.

"You know Charlotte, Mama used to have a crush on Jack Black, who plays Bowser," She told her as they got popcorn and drinks at the movie theater, "The theaters are so nice nowadays."

"Ew, gross, keep that to yourself!" Charlotte exclaimed.

She did like Princess Peach, so they all wore their matching Mario shirts that day.

They all loved the movie, and Charlotte was pleased. So Mama moved forward with surprising them with her Easter plans. Funnily enough, Charlotte's favorite present was a cheap squishmellow cat from 5 below, which Mama got last minute as Build a Bear was all out of Princess Peach Bunny outfits.

"I also got us Universal Studio Annual passes! We'll go as a family for my birthday."

Mama thought this would be perfect. She planned to propose at Toadstool Café like years ago in Santa Barbara on June 3rd, to be exact. Little did she know, this was the idea I planted for Bentley to get his dog wings and join us for good in heaven.

Finally, it was June. Charlotte had been to Universal before for her birthday but was not a fan anymore. "This place sucks!" she said. She had brought her new stuffed cat, which she named Nay Nay.

Papa brought the Super Nintendo Switch to play Mario games as they waited in Bowser's castle for the new ride.

Mama was happiest. However, she couldn't help but remember how angry she was at Papa, who gave her classic Nintendo games to Demon Brent right before they first split up without telling her. While in line, Mama called Toadstool café.

"You can't go in," Papa warned her as he played his Switch. You have to make a reservation ahead of time.

Mama called the number and, unfortunately, was denied, saying they were all booked for the day. 'What?!' She got a text to watch the Mario movie on her cell phone instead. When she called, she could hear Luigi Charlie Day's voice on the phone. "Sorry, we are unavailable. If you're having a plumbing emergency, please leave your number, and we will get back to you soon."

Suddenly, Mama's heart was pounding as she felt overwhelmed with nervousness. She could feel herself getting dizzy, and everything went dark.

Mama could hear a familiar voice. Her eyes opened, her surroundings cleared, and she felt like she was in some strange hospital room. She saw Demon Brent in front of her. She almost screamed when she saw him. Her heart raced as she recognized the face. Her initial shock was replaced with a pleasant surprise.

"Brent, what are you doing here?" she inquired, her voice a mix of confusion and curiosity.

He offered a small, reassuring smile. "You fainted at Universal Studios," he explained, "They called me, so I rushed over as soon as I heard. You're in their first aid room."

Mama's mind was still trying to make sense of the situation. Then, her brow furrowed. "Where's Roy? Where's Charlotte?" she asked.

Demon Brent's eyes sparkled mischievously. "Oh, they're waiting outside," he replied, "But before we get into that, I have some amazing news for you!"

Just as Mama tried to inquire further, the door swung open, and walked in no other than Dave Grohl. Her surprise multiplied as her gaze shifted from Brent to the rock legend who had walked in through the door.

"Oh my gosh! Dave Grohl! What are you doing here?!" she exclaimed, her astonishment evideDrnt in her voice.

Dave let out a hearty chuckle and gave her his charming smile, his easy-going demeanor putting everyone at ease. "Well, Brent here is going to be my new drummer for the Foo Fighters!" he announced with pizzazz.

Mama's eyes widened, and a gasp escaped her lips. She turned her attention back to Brent; he was just as surprised as she was. Without warning, Brent let out an exuberant whoop and jumped into the air, unable to contain his excitement.

The room was filled with a mixture of emotions; surprise, happiness, and disbelief.

"Oh my god, Brent!" Mama exclaimed, clapping her hands in exhilaration, "This is incredible news! I am so happy for you!"

Dave Grohl stood near the bed, watching the scene unfold with a grin on his face. The atmosphere in the room was electric as the weight of the revelation sank in.

"Brent! You're gonna be so famous!" Mama cried, her voice brimming with pride and admiration.

Brent's face broke into another wide smile, and his excitement was palpable. "Yes!" he exclaimed. The idea of becoming known to the world and sharing his musical talent seemed to light up his entire being. Mama could sense the adrenaline coursing through his veins. At that moment, she could not have been happier for him. This unexpected turn of events brought a wave of joy. She got up and hugged Brent.

Dave Grohl's presence added an element of surrealism to the scene, making it a memory that Mama and Brent would cherish for years to come.

"There is a catch, however," said Dave, breaking the celebration.

"What is that?" inquired Mama.

"Ashley, you have to marry Charlie Day!" said Dave.

Before she could react, the door swung open again, and in walked Charlie Day dressed as Luigi with a bouquet of beautiful Mario Fire Power flowers. Mama could not believe her eyes. "Charlie Day?!" she exclaimed.

"Yes, Ashley," he said, "I saw you outside Bowser's castle and knew you were the woman for me. I asked Roy for his blessing. He is okay as long as he doesn't have to pay child support."

"You know what? I believe this is fate!" said Mama, "I love you too, Charlie Day!"

"Yaay!" everyone cheered.

He then picked her up from the hospital bed in a romantic swoop and carried her outside.

Waiting for them was a magical Mario pipe, which they jumped into, and it took them to Rainbow Road World.

Jack Black, in his Bowser outfit, was waiting for them, chosen to conduct the wedding ceremony. All the Mario characters were there, Luigi and Daisy, along with actors Chris Pratt voicing Mario and Seth Rogan voicing Donkey Kong, all waited for them as Mama and Charlie Day were magically changed into beautiful wedding suits and dresses, mesmerizing the crowd sparkling against the rainbow lights.

Big Boo and Toad shouted out happily as Princess Peach, an honorary bridesmaid, walked down the aisle holding Charlotte's hand as she cried. "No, I don't want my mom to marry him!" she said through the tears.

Jack Black began to speak, "Thank you all for coming today to see these two beautiful souls become joined together as one. If there is anyone who objects to this wedding, speak now or forever hold your peace."

"We object!" yelled some familiar hateful voices.

All of a sudden, Laura, Demon Brent's wife, stepped out of the crowd with Satan Nic, the Gromefiels bassist from hell.

"IM THE PLUMBER, NOT CHARLIE DAY!" he yelled, "I was her contact For Plumbing emergencies. THIS WEDDING IS AN INJUSTICE!"

A beautiful, menacing sound arose, drowning out their screams. It was Kyle Gass from Tenacious D who played the guitar solo that called a large Mario bullet to hit Laura and summon a group of Koopas to take Satan Nic to Bowser's Dungeon.

Chris Pratt laughed, "That guy has had too many toadstool mushrooms."

Aubrey Plaza randomly rode in on Yoshi, yelling "France!" from her SNL sketch as the crowd cheered.

Meanwhile, sweating and breaking out in hives, Mama and Charlie Day struggled through the awkward ceremony holding hands.

After the vows were read and the wedding rings were exchanged, Jack Black said, "Now take these Negan's bats and throw them in the crowd!"

Suddenly, the rapper Machine Gun Kelly came out of the crowd, singing his Twin Flame song. "This song goes out to Charlie and Ashley," he yelled to the flailing crowd.

Bentley came out of the flames now as Bowser's castle was in the background. He was floating in the air, playing the guitar solo.

I could no longer hold my anger watching this from my cloud, drinking my martini. "Lexi, hold my drink," I said and handed it to her. I then motioned for Lakitu, the evil cloud guy, to take me to this ridiculous ceremony. "Hang this dog treat for that dumb Demon Dog Bentley!" I yelled to him, "he will fall for it."

We floated down, and the flames were fogging evil cloud guy Lakitu's glasses, but it didn't stop us. Bentley saw us, and as I predicted, he started doing his dumb dance. We lowered the treat to him, which he grabbed with his mouth. I screamed, jumping off the cloud.

"You are a bad influence; no twin flame here!" I simultaneously slapped Bentley and Machine Gun Kelly with my paw.

"Papa, you cheap bastard!" I continued, "You have no morals, Papa, what are you doing? Take care of Mama! You would agree to this to not pay child support ?!"

"Damn you, Bentley, and your stupid twin flame bullshit psychology. Evil shit! Go back to hell, Bentley!" I yelled.

Bentley and Papa hung their heads down in shame.

"Wake up, Mama!" screamed a little girl's voice that shattered the scene unfolding in front of Mama. She woke up in a hospital bed (again). Papa and Charlotte were there this time, watching her with concern.

"Wh-what happened?" she asked.

"Oh, you slipped and fell outside Toadstool Café and hit your head, but you're okay," said Papa. He handed her some water.

"Oh, I had the strangest dream!" said Mama, "I was going to marry Charlie Day!"

"Keep dreaming, haha!" laughed Papa.

"I hate this place!" Charlotte screamed, diverting her parents' attention toward her. "Let's go home!" she protested. They did ride Bowser's Mario Kart ride at least.

As the sun began to set, casting a warm orange glow over the city, Mama's disappointment for not being able to get her favorite butterbeer at Harry Potter World and her proposal Plan disaster started to dissipate. Driving through the streets of Encino, Papa had a surprise for her.

They pulled up to Mel's Diner, and the familiar neon sign flickered to life against the orange sky. Mama's eyes widened in pleasant shock; her lips curved into a faint smile. It was like stepping into the past when they went inside the diner. Papa led them to a corner booth, and they settled in. As the waitress came to them with a menu, Mama already knew what she wanted. She got herself their signature Lana Del Rey-inspired shakes without hesitation. She and Papa are still saddened when they missed her concert with Courtney Love years ago. They had tickets and drove three hours from San Luis Obispo but couldn't find parking.

Mama lovingly looked into the eyes of the two people she called her family. She was touched by Roy's thoughtfulness.

As the evening continued, laughter and conversation flowed freely between the three, and many stories and jokes were exchanged. Memories were revisited, and the bonds between them grew even stronger. As they left the diner at night, their hearts and stomachs were full, bringing a sense of contentment to them. The smiles were a testament to how much they had enjoyed themselves due to such a simple gesture from Papa.

"Thank you, guys! This is the best birthday ever!" Mama exclaimed as she shared her Lana Del Rey shake with her loved ones. They all sang along to their jukebox playing "Video Games," laughing.

Lexi and I watched down happily, singing with them.

Chapter 11: Hope on the Horizon

"Wallace, it's Bentley on the phone again. He wants to speak to you."

"No, thank you, Lexi. I don't want to speak to him."

"Wallace, it's been weeks. Just hear his side of the story. Just try."

"Fine, I'll do it for you, Lexi," I said as I grabbed the phone, "What is it, Bentley? What do you have to say for yourself for that hell spectacle?"

"I'm angry too, Wallace. Not at you or Lexi, but at Papa and Mama's friends and family... I don't like that Mama is always proposing to Papa, and he keeps hurting her, saying 'no' because he doesn't love her. She doesn't deserve to be hurt like this over and over. The worst thing is that he also controls her. He has no right to do so. They shouldn't be treating her that way. I agree with the psychiatrists that it's them and not her ."

My ears turned slightly, "So you have decided to give up on getting them back together? I know Papa is not perfect, but he always loved you, Bentley. Remember when you bit his lip and put him in the hospital? Most owners would have put you down. Instead, he loved you still. Come on, Bentley! Come on, get serious now. What kind of an unloyal poodle you are to Papa right now?"

"You were right, Wallace. I will not do that again. I will be on team De La O. Let's just plan another proposal. This time, let's get Papa to see the error of his ways with the ghosts of dogs from the past on Christmas Eve."

"Hmmm, I like your thinking, Bentley. Look, let's do plan B. Christmas is coming, and you can torture Papa. I still have hope."

"I'm sorry, Wallace. I hope you can forgive me."

"Okay, I forgive you, my friend. Let's move forward with your plan."

"Thank you, Wallace. Good night, and don't let the bed bugs bite."

I laughed, "I love you, Bentley."

"I love you too, Wallace."

Lexi brought me my treats and slippers. She smiled, hearing us as she approached the scene, "I'm glad you are speaking to each other again."

"Me too, Lexi. I love that crazy canine. Even though he makes me want to bite him and teach him a lesson."

I hung up the phone feeling a little better. I realized Bentley was expressing his anger and frustration seeing his owner being abused and mistreated by so many friends and family members. I understood where he was coming from and why he would rather be in hell with Satan, but there was hope still, as I did not want to give up on Bentley getting his doggy wings and getting our family back together again.

The weight of the situation bore down on me, but there was a glimmer of hope in Bentley's actions. It had been a difficult journey for both of us, and I couldn't help but reflect on how this all started.

Bentley, my loyal friend and a loving dog, had always been an integral part of our family. With time, he became frustrated as he saw the treatment his owner was going through. Bentley's anger was a manifestation of his loyalty and his way of saying, "I won't stand by while they hurt Mama."

I sat down, contemplating Bentley's profound connection to Mama. His anger was justified. It was a surreal thought, imagining the faithful dog in the depths of the underworld because his love knew no bounds.

Despite the pain and the turmoil that had entered our lives, a glimmer of hope remained. I refused to give up on the idea of Bentley earning his doggy wings and our family being reunited. So, with renewed determination, I decided that it was time to mend the broken relationships and find the strength to confront the demon bassists Sarah and Satan Nic that had torn our family apart.

I hugged Lexi as I stared at our various family photos through the years. My favorite one of me, Mama, Papa, and Bentley that we took at Picture People at the mall. Another of Charlotte and us at her first Christmas meeting with Santa and Mrs. Clause at a beautiful farm we went to visit near Atascadero. Lexi with my girls and me when they were born, Mama holding all of us beaming. Me with Charlotte, Grandpa, and the Easter Bunny in Palateen, most recently before my passing. I even had a photo of Evil Grandma. I pictured Mama and Papa dancing together in the warm golden light of the evening, their feet floating above the air and barely touching the ground. Their love was a melody that echoed through a meadow. Each step brought them closer to one another.

As I yawned, my hope-filled daydreams began to weave a story of Mama and Papa being reunited. I imagined that their love was a lighthouse guiding them through the stormy seas of life, steering them back into each other's arms. Wrapped snugly in my blanket, I closed my eyes and drifted off into the world of dreams and yearning.

Made in the USA
Las Vegas, NV
28 October 2023

79841890R00072